PENGUIN BOOKS

HAPPY TO BE HERE

Garrison Keillor was born in Anoka, Minnesota, in 1942 and has been in broadcasting since 1960, most of that time with Minnesota Public Radio. In 1974, in addition to his regular morning show, he began a weekly program of live music and humor called "A Prairie Home Companion," featuring reports from the fictional town of Lake Wobegon, Minnesota, "where all the women are strong, all the men good-looking, and all the children above average." It can now be heard on 202 stations over American Public Radio, and in 1980 it won a George Foster Peabody Award for distinguished broadcasting. Garrison Keillor's writing has appeared in *The New Yorker* for more than ten years, as well as in *The Atlantic Monthly*, the *Los Angeles Times*, the *Minneapolis Tribune*, and several other publications. He has one son and lives in St. Paul.

Garrison Keillor

Happy to

Be Here

Penguin Books

Penguin Books Ltd, Harmondsworth,
Middlesex, England
Penguin Books, 40 West 23rd Street,
New York, New York 10010, U.S.A.
Penguin Books Australia Ltd, Ringwood,
Victoria, Australia
Penguin Books Canada Limited, 2801 John Street,
Markham, Ontario, Canada L3R 1B4
Penguin Books (N.Z.) Ltd, 182–190 Wairau Road,
Auckland 10, New Zealand

First published in the United States of America by
Atheneum Publishers 1981
First published in Canada by
McClelland and Stewart Limited 1981
Published in Penguin Books in slightly different order
and with five new stories—"The Tip-Top Club," "Jack
Schmidt on the Burning Sands," "The New Washington:
An Inside Story," "My Stepmother, Myself," and "After a
Fall"—1983

LIBRARY OF CONGRESS CATALOGING IN PUBLICATION DATA
Keillor, Garrison.
    Happy to be here.
    I. Title.
PS3561.E3755H3   1983   813'.54   82-12281
ISBN 0 14 00.6482 6

Printed in the United States of America by
R.R. Donnelley & Sons Company, Harrisonburg, Virginia
Set in Video Garamond

All stories in *Happy to Be Here* appeared originally in *The New Yorker*,
with the exceptions of "The Tip-Top Club," "Jack Schmidt on the Burn-
ings Sands," "My Stepmother, Myself," "Shy Rights: Why Not Pretty
Soon?," "Your Transit Commission," and "The Drunkard's Sunday." "The
Tip-Top Club," "My Stepmother, Myself," and "Your Transit Commission" appeared originally in *The Atlantic Monthly*. "Jack Schmidt on the
Burning Sands" appeared originally in *Twin Cities*. "Happy to Be Here"
appeared in *The New Yorker* under the title "Found Paradise."

CONTENTS

3

4

5

INTRODUCTION

All but six of these stories appeared in *The New Yorker* between 1969 and 1982; all were written here in Minnesota, many of them in the front bedroom of an old stucco house in St. Paul, where I used to keep an unfinished novel. It lay on a shelf over the radiator, and next to it stood the typewriter stand, up against a window that looked out on an elm tree and a yellow bungalow with blue trim, across the street. I assume it was an elm because it died that spring during an elm epidemic and the city foresters cut it down, but in fact there are only four or five plants I can identify with certainty and the elm is not one of them. I regret this but there it is: plant life has never been more to me than a sort of canvas backdrop. There was a houseplant in that bedroom, too, some type of vine or vine-related plant, and it also died.

I'd say that personal ignorance was the chief inspiration of that poor novel, the shelf novel, and was the main cause of its lingering death that summer, including ignorance of plants. In a novel, characters shouldn't lean against "a tree"—it ought to be a specific tree (e.g., birch, maple, oak), just as when a character feels bad it ought not be a vague sense of uneasiness but something definitely *wrong* and the writer should say what. An impacted molar, too much beer at the ball game, fear of spiders, or *what*.

In my shelf novel, all the guys were marathon leaners. They leaned against vague vegetation and felt vaguely ill and unhappy, probably the result of their getting no exercise and smoking so many cigarettes. They smoked cigarettes like some people use semicolons:

> "I'm not sure, not sure at all—" he lit a cigarette and inhaled deeply—"perhaps I never will."

After the elm died, the yellow bungalow was in clear view, and I began to notice a fat boy who spent most of his sunny afternoons sitting on the front steps, smoking Marlboros and drinking Gatorade. He had long blond hair styled after Farrah Fawcett's, and weighed a lot. He was fourteen, a neighbor lady told me, and his name was Curtis. Every afternoon he hove into view and plopped down and proceeded to while away the hours watching traffic, and by June, when school ended and he added a morning appearance, he was getting on my nerves.

He was a nice boy, the neighbor said, was kind to children, including my own, and had every right to take the load off his feet, and I had no right to expect he should run around with other boys who probably made fun of him, but I did wish he would do something. Read books. When I was fourteen, I was happy to read all day every day and into the night. I hid in closets and in the basement, locked myself in the bathroom, reading right up to the final moment when Mother pried the book from my fingers and shoved me outdoors into the land of living persons.

She was right to do that. If she hadn't, I would be four feet tall, have beady little eyes and a caved-in chest and a butt like a bushel basket.

Boys stopped by the steps and talked to Curtis, he was no social outcast. From the typewriter I noticed plenty of visits: skinny kids in shorts, boys Curtis's age. At that age, kids are in constant motion even when they stop and talk. They shift from foot to foot, pick tufts of grass and throw them at each other, sit down, jump up, poke each other, kick stones, but not Curtis, he was set in concrete. The boys moved on, he stayed put, smoked his cigarettes, kept his hair in place.

I could have moved the typewriter away from the window and put Curtis and his problems behind me, and yet the novel in front of me was no great shakes either and, in many ways, less interesting than Curtis. Characters came into that novel, looked around for a few pages, and jumped ship.

> Suddenly he decided to go to France. He had never been to France. France sounded pretty good to him. "Going to France," he said. She lit a cigarette and inhaled deeply. "You said that before," she said sardonically. But this time was different. This time he actually went. She was really surprised, but there was no doubt about it. He was in France. "I may never see him again," she thought, and she was right. She never did.

Meanwhile, at the bungalow, Curtis's mom and dad emerged. She was pretty and probably a terrific cook, by the look of things. The dad was—how can you put this gracefully?—a real blimp, a wide load, and the white polyester stretch-pants only emphasized the cargo. He tapped Curtis on the head, and the three of them got into their white Imperial. The adjustable steering wheel moved forward, the dad slid in, and the car moved off like a dirigible loosed from the mooring mast. I guessed they were going out to eat and not to a restaurant with a lot of sunlight and plants and spinach salads. A joint where the plates are like platters, where the light is dim and a big person can take on a cow, no questions asked.

I could have quit the novel and put it in a box; it was going nowhere. In fact I quit the novel almost every day, put it in a box, wrote more novel and put *that* in the box. I wished my mother would come, rip the paper out of the carriage, and make me go play tennis. What kept me beating on the novel was the sheer size of it and of my investment in it; this was no birdhouse I had screwed up but a genuine mansion, a three-story plaster-of-paris mansion deluxe designed by me and propped up by hundreds of two-by-fours; a fellow doesn't walk away from a mistake that big, he likes to keep at it; he thinks that maybe the addition of one more two-by-four will solve the problem.

Meanwhile, I wrote these stories.

I've been reluctant to collect them in a book because they were written in revolt against a book and out of admiration for a magazine, *The New Yorker*, which I first saw in 1956 in the Anoka Public Library. Our family subscribed to *Reader's Digest*, *Popular Mechanics*, *National Geographic*, *Boys' Life*, and *American Home*. My people weren't much for literature, and they were dead set against conspicuous wealth, so a magazine in which classy paragraphs marched down the aisle between columns of diamond necklaces and French cognacs was not a magazine they welcomed into their home. I was more easily dazzled than they and to me *The New Yorker* was a fabulous sight, an immense glittering ocean liner off the coast of Minnesota, and I loved to read it. I bought copies and smuggled them home, though with a clear conscience, for what I most admired was not the decor or the tone of the thing but rather the work of some writers, particularly *The New Yorker*'s great infield of Thurber, Liebling, Perelman, and White.

They were my heroes: four older gentlemen, one blind, one fat, one delicate, and one a chicken rancher, and in my mind they took the field against the big mazumbos of American Literature, and I cheered for them. I cheer for them now, all dead except Mr. White, and still think (as I thought then) that it is more worthy in the eyes of God and better for us as a people if a writer make three pages sharp and funny about the lives of geese than to make three hundred flat and flabby about God or the American people.

I worked on the novel all summer. Curtis came out and sat on the steps morning and afternoon during August, then school started and he appeared only in the afternoon. Slowly it occurred to me that I was only sitting around, and though a person would like to think that ambition counts for something, the truth is that it doesn't. There is no difference between a fat boy lounging on the steps and a man at a typewriter turning out horseshit writing. No difference at all. Not in this world or the next.

I kept the cardboard boxful of novel, thinking I wanted some evidence in case there *is* a difference, then decided to throw it away. I was in the midst of a divorce and was divesting myself of all sorts of possessions, and threw the novel into the back of a truck along with some other trash, and never thought about it until thinking about this book.

Curtis has lost a lot of weight, the neighbor lady tells me, and is doing quite well at the University of Minnesota where he is majoring in plant pathology. He is married. My stucco house is still there. My boy is twelve years old. This book is dedicated to him.

Happy to Be Here

1

JACK SCHMIDT,
ARTS ADMINISTRATOR

It was one of those sweltering days toward the end of the fiscal year when Minneapolis smells of melting asphalt and foundation money is as tight as a rusted nut. Ninety-six, the radio said on the way in from the airport, and back at my office in the Acme Building I was trying to fan the memory of ocean breezes in Hawaii, where I had just spent two days attending a conference on midwestern regionalism.

It wasn't working. I was sitting down, jacket off, feet up, looking at the business end of an air conditioner, and a numb spot was forming around my left ear to which I was holding a telephone and listening to Bobby Jo, my secretary at the Twin Cities Arts Mall, four blocks away, reading little red numerals off a sheet of paper. We had only two days before the books snapped shut, and our administrative budget had sprung a deficit big enough to drive a car through—a car full of accountants.

I could feel a dark sweat stain spreading across the back of my best blue shirt.

"Listen," I sputtered, "I still got some loose bucks in the publicity budget. Let's transfer that to administration."

"J.S.," she sighed, "I just got done telling you. Those loose bucks are as spent as an octogenarian after an all-night bender. Right now we're using more red ink than the funny papers, and yesterday we bounced three checks right off the bottom of the account. That budget is so unbalanced, it's liable to go out and shoot somebody."

You could've knocked me over with a rock.

"Sweetheart," I lied quietly, hoping she couldn't hear my heavy breathing, "don't worry about it. Old Jack has been around the block once or twice. I'll straighten it out."

"Payday is tomorrow," she sniffed sharply. "Twelve noon."

The Arts Mall is just one of thirty-seven arts organizations I administer, a chain that stretches from the Anaheim Puppet Theatre to the Title IX Poetry Center in Bangor, and I could have let it go down the tubes, but hell, I kind of like the joint. It's an old Henny Penny supermarket that we renovated in 1976 when Bicentennial money was wandering around like helpless buffalo, and it houses seventeen little shops—mainly pottery and macrame, plus a dulcimer-maker, a printmaker, a spatter painter, two sculptors, and a watering hole called The Barre. This is one of those quiet little bistros where you aren't driven crazy by the constant ringing of cash registers. A nice place to drink but you wouldn't want to own it.

I hung up the phone and sat for a few minutes eyeballing an old nine-by-twelve glossy of myself, trying to get inspired. It's not a bad likeness. Blue pin-striped suit, a headful of hair, and I'm looking straight into 1965 like I owned it, and as for my line of work at the time, anyone who has read *The Blonde in*

204, *Close Before Striking*, *The Big Tipper*, and *The Mark of a Heel* knows that I wasn't big on ballet.

I wasn't real smart at spotting trends, either. The private-eye business was getting thinner than sliced beef at the deli. I spent my days supporting a bookie and my nights tailing guys who weren't going anywhere anyway. My old pals in Homicide were trading in their wing tips and porkpie hats for Frye boots and Greek fisherman caps and growing big puffs of hair around their ears. Mine was the only suit that looked slept in. I felt like writing to the Famous Shamus School and asking what was I doing wrong.

"It's escapism, Mr. Schmidt," quavered Ollie, the elevator boy, one morning when I complained that nobody needed a snoop anymore. "I was reading in the *Gazette* this morning where they say this is an age of anti-intellectualism. A sleuth like yourself, now, you represent the spirit of inquiry, the scientific mind, eighteenth-century enlightenment, but heck, people don't care about knowing the truth anymore. They just want to have *experiences*."

"Thanks for the tip, Ollie," I smiled, flipping him a quarter. "And keep your eyes open."

I was having an experience myself at the time and her name was Trixie, an auburn-haired beauty who moved grown men to lie down in her path and wave their arms and legs. I was no stronger than the rest, and when she let it be known one day that the acting studio where she studied nights was low on cash and might have to close and thus frustrate her career, I didn't ask her to type it in triplicate. I got the dough. I learned then and there that true artists are sensitive about money. Trixie took the bundle and the next day she moved in with a sandal-maker. She said I wasn't her type. Too materialistic.

Evidently I was just the type that every art studio, mime troupe, print gallery, folk-ballet company, and wind ensemble in town was looking for, though, and the word got around fast: Jack Schmidt knows how to dial a telephone and make big checks arrive in the mail. Pretty soon my outer office was full of people with long delicate fingers, waiting to tell me what marvelous, marvelous things they could do if only they had ten thousand dollars (minus my percentage). It didn't take me long to learn the rules—about twenty minutes. First rule: ten thousand is peanuts. Pocket money. Any arts group that doesn't need a hundred grand and need it *now* just isn't thinking hard enough.

My first big hit was a National Endowment for the Arts grant for a walk-up tap school run by a dishwater blonde named Bonnie Marie Beebe. She also taught baton, but we stressed tap on the application. We called the school The American Conservatory of Jazz Dance. A hundred and fifty thousand clams. "Seed money" they called it, but it was good crisp lettuce to me.

I got the Guild of Younger Poets fifty thousand from the Teamsters to produce some odes to the open road, and another fifteen from a lumber tycoon with a yen for haiku. I got a yearlong folk-arts residency for a guy who told Scandinavian jokes, and I found wealthy backers for a play called *Struck by Lightning*, by a non-literalist playwright who didn't write a script but only spoke with the director a few times on the phone.

Nobody was too weird for Jack Schmidt. In every case, I had met weirder on the street. The Minnesota Anti-Dance Ensemble, for example, is a bunch of sweet kids. They simply don't believe in performance. They say that "audience" is a passive concept, and they spend a lot of time picketing large corporations in protest against the money that has been given to them, which they say comes from illicit profits. It doesn't make my life easier, but heck, I was young once, too. Give me a choice, I'll take a radical dance group over a Renaissance-music ensemble any day. Your average shawm or sackbut player thinks the world owes him a goddamn living.

So I was off the pavement and into the arts, and one day Bobby Jo walked in, fresh out of St. Cloud State Normal and looking for money to teach interior decorating to minority kids, and she saw I needed her more. She threw out my electric fan and the file cabinet with the half-empty fifth in the third drawer and brought in some Mondrian prints and a glass-topped desk and about forty potted plants. She took away my .38 and made me switch to filter cigarettes and had stationery printed up that looks like it's recycled from beaten eggs. "Arts Consultant," it says, but what I sell is the same old hustle and muscle, which was a new commodity on the arts scene then.

"What your arts organizations need is a guy who can ask people for large amounts without blushing and twisting his hankie," I told her one day, en route to Las Palmas for a three-day seminar on the role of the arts in rural America. "Your typical general manager of an arts organization today is nothing but a bagman. He figures all he has to do is pass the hat at the board meeting and the Throttlebottoms will pick up the deficit. The rest of the time he just stands around at lawn parties and says witty things. But the arts are changing, Bobby Jo. Nowadays, everybody wants arts, not just the rich. It's big business. Operating budgets are going right through the ceiling. All of a sudden, Mr. Arts Guy finds the game has changed. Now he has to work for the money and hit up corporations and think box office and dive in and fight for a slice of the government pie, and it scares him right out of his silk jammies. That's when he calls for Schmidt."

She slipped her hand into mine. I didn't take her pulse or anything, but I could tell she was excited by the way her breath came in quick little gasps.

"Now anyone who can spell 'innovative' can apply for a grant, government or otherwise," I went on, "but that doesn't mean that the bozo who reads the application is necessarily going to bust into tears and run right down to Western Union. He needs some extra incentive. He needs to know that this is no idle request for funds typed up by somebody who happened to find a blank application form at the post office. He needs to know that you are counting on the cash, that you fully expect to get it, and that if you are denied you are capable of putting his fingers in a toaster. The arts are growing, Bobby Jo, and you and me are going to make it happen."

"You are a visionary, J.S.," she murmured. "You have a tremendous overall concept but you need a hand when it comes to the day-to-day."

"Speaking of ideas," I muttered hoarsely, and I pulled the lap blanket up over our heads. She whispered my initials over and over in a litany of passion. I grabbed her so hard her ribs squeaked.

It was a rough morning. After Bobby Jo's phone call, I got another from the Lawston Foundry, informing me that Stan Lewandowski's sculpture, *Oppresso,* would not be cast in time for the opening of the Minot Performing Arts Center. The foundry workers, after hearing what Lewandowski was being paid for creating what looked to them like a large gerbil cage, went out on strike, bringing the sculpture to a standstill. I wasted fifteen minutes trying to make a lunch date with Hugo Groveland, the mining heir, to discuss the Arts Mall. He was going away for a while, Groveland said, and didn't know when he'd be back, if ever. He hinted at dark personal tragedies that were haunting him and suggested I call his mother. "She's more your type," he said, "plus she's about to kick off, if you know what I mean."

On top of it, I got a call from the director of our dinner theatre in upstate Indiana. He had been irked at me for weeks since I put the kibosh on *Hedda Gabler.* He had been plumping for a repertory theatre. "Fine," I said. "As long as you make it *Fiddler on the Roof, The Sunshine Boys,* and *Man of La Mancha.*"

Now he was accusing us of lacking a commitment to new writers. He said I was in the business of exploiting talent, not developing it.

"Listen, pal," I snarled. "As a director, you'd have a hard time getting people to act normal. So don't worry about me exploiting your talent. Just make sure you have as many people in the cast as there are parts. And tell your kitchen to slice the roast beef thin."

So he quit. I wished I could, too. I had a headache that wouldn't. And an Arts Mall with twenty-four hours to live.

"It's a whole trend called the New Naiveté," offered Ollie when I asked him why artists seemed to hate me, on the way down to lunch. "I was reading in the *Gazette* where they say people nowadays think simplicity is a prime virtue. They want to eliminate the middleman. That's you, Mr. Schmidt. Traditionally, your role has been that of a buffer between the individual and a cruel world. But now people think the world is kind and good, if only they could deal with it directly. They think if they got rid of the middleman—the bureaucracy, whatever you call it—then everything would be hunky-dory."

"Thanks, Ollie," I said as the elevator doors opened. "Let's have lunch sometime."

It reminded me of something Bobby Jo had said in a taxicab in Rio, where we were attending a five-day conference on the need for a comprehensive system of evaluating arts information. "It's simple, J.S.," she said. "The problem is overhead. Your fat cats will give millions to build an arts center, but nobody wants to donate to pay the light bill because you can't put a plaque on it. They'll pay for Chippewa junk sculpture, but who wants to endow the janitor?"

"Speaking of endowments," I whispered hoarsely, and I leaned over and pressed my lips hungrily against hers. I could feel her earlobes trembling helplessly.

The mining heir's mother lived out on Mississippi Drive in a stone pile the size of the Lincoln Monument and about as cheerful. The carpet in the hall was so deep it was like walking through a swamp. The woman who opened the door eyeballed me carefully for infectious diseases, then led me to a sitting room on the second floor that could've gone straight into the Cooper-Hewitt Museum. Mrs. Groveland sat in a wing chair by the fireplace. She looked pretty good for a woman who was about to make the far turn.

"Mr. Smith, how good of you to come," she tooted, offering me a tiny hand. I didn't correct her on the name. For a few grand, I'm willing to be called a lot worse. "Sit down and tell me about your arts center," she continued. "I'm all ears."

So were the two Dobermans who sat on either side of her chair. They looked as if they were trained to rip your throat if you used the wrong fork.

Usually, my pitch begins with a description of the long lines of art-starved inner-city children bused in daily to the Arts Mall to be broadened. But the hounds made me nervous—they maintained the most intense eye contact I had ever seen from floor level—so I skipped ahead to the money part. I dropped the figure of fifty thousand dollars.

She didn't blink, so I started talking about the Mall's long-range needs. I mentioned a hundred thou. She smiled as if I had asked for a drink of water.

I crossed my legs and forged straight ahead. "Mrs. Groveland," I radiated. "I hope you won't mind if I bring up the subject of estate planning."

"Of course not," she radiated right back. "The bulk of my estate, aside from the family bequests and a lump-sum gift to the Audubon Society, is going for the care of Luke and Mona here." At the word "estate," the Dobermans seemed to lick their chops.

I had to think fast. I wasn't about to bad-mouth our feathered friends of the forest, or Mrs. Groveland's family, either, but I thought I just might shake loose some of the dog trust. I told her about our Founders Club for contributors of fifty thousand or more. Perhaps she could obtain *two* Founderships—one for each Doberman. "Perhaps it would take a load off your mind if you would let us provide for Luke and Mona," I said. "We could act as their trustees. We just happen to have this lovely Founders Club Kennel, way out in the country, where—"

At the mention of a kennel, the beasts lowered their heads and growled. Their eyes never left my face.

"Hush, hush," Mrs. Groveland scolded gently. "Don't worry," she assured me, "they don't bite."

They may not bite, I thought, but they can sue.

Then Mona barked. Instantly, I was on my feet, but the dogs beat me to it. The sounds that came from their throats were noises that predated the Lascaux Cave paintings. They were the cries of ancient Doberman souls trying to break through the thin crust of domestication, and they expressed a need that was far deeper than that of the Arts Mall, the arts in general, or any individual artist whom I would care to know. The next sound I heard was the slam of a paneled oak door closing. I was out in the hallway and I could hear Mrs. Groveland on the other side saying, "*Bad* Luke, *naughty* Mona!" The woman who had let me in let me out. "They're quite protective," she informed me, chuckling. If a jury had been there to see her face, I'd have altered it.

When I got back to the office, I gathered up every piece of correspondence in our National Arts Endowment file and threw it out the window. From above, it looked like a motorcade was due any minute. I was about to follow up with some of the potted plants when the phone rang. It rang sixteen times before I picked it up. Before Bobby Jo could identify herself, I'd used up all the best words I know. "I'm *out*," I added. "Through. Done. Kaput. Fini. The End. Cue the creditors. I've had it."

"J.S.," she began, but I was having none of it.

"I've had a noseful of beating money out of bushes so a bunch of sniveling wimps can try the patience of tiny audiences of their pals and moms with subsidized garbage that nobody in his right mind would pay Monopoly money to see," I snapped. "I'm sick of people calling themselves artists who make pots that cut your fingers when you pick them up and wobble when you set them on a table. I'm tired of poets who dribble out little teensy poems in lower-case letters and I'm sick of painters who can't even draw an outline of their own hand and I'm finished with the mumblers and stumblers who tell you that if you don't understand them it's *your* fault."

I added a few more categories to my list, plus a couple dozen persons by name, several organizations, and a breed of dog.

"You all done, J.S.?" she asked. "Because I've got great news. The Highways Department is taking the Arts Mall for an interchange. They're ready to pay top dollar, plus—you won't believe this—to sweeten the deal, they're throwing in six point two miles of Interstate 594."

"Miles of what?" Then it clicked. "You mean that unfinished leg of 594?" I choked.

"It's been sitting there for years. There are so many community groups opposed to it that the Highways Department doesn't dare cut the grass that's growing on it. They want us to take them off the hook. And if we make it an arts space, they figure it'll fulfill their beautification quota for the next three years."

"We'll call it The ArtsTrip!" I exclaimed. "Or The ArtStrip! The median as medium! Eight-lane environmental art! Big, big sculptures! Action painting! Wayside dance areas! Living poetry plaques! Milestones in American music! Arts parks and Arts lots! A drive-in film series! The customized car as American genre! The customized van as Artsmobile! People can have an arts experience without even pulling over onto the shoulder. They can get quality enrichment and still make good time!"

"Speaking of making time—" Her voice broke. She shuddered like a turned-on furnace. Her breath came in sudden little sobs.

I don't know what's next for Jack Schmidt after the Arts Highway is finished, but, whatever it is, it's going to have Jack Schmidt's name on it. No more Mr. Anonymous for me. No more Gray Eminence trips for yours truly. A couple of days ago, I was sitting at my desk and I began fooling around with an ink pad. I started making thumbprints on a sheet of yellow paper and then I sort of smooshed them around a little, and one thing led to another, and when I got done with it I liked what I saw. It wasn't necessarily something I'd hang on a burlap wall with a baby ceiling-spot aimed at it, but it had a certain *definite* quality that art could use a lot more of. I wouldn't be too surprised if in my next adventure I'm in a loft in SoHo solving something strictly visual while Bobby Jo throws me smoldering looks from her loom in the corner. In the meantime, good luck and stay out of dark alleys.

- stray from to
- general overview
- resolving an issue

DON: THE TRUE STORY
OF A YOUNG PERSON

Earl and Mavis Beeman and son Don, seventeen, had lived together in the two-bedroom green-stucco house at 2813 Rochester for sixteen years, but for the last two they had been like ships in the night. Don, a gangly youth with his father's large head and flat nose and his mother's shoulder-length hair, kept to himself and seldom spoke unless spoken to. "Ever since he joined that band . . ." his dad said. Mavis suspected drugs and finally asked Don straight out. He told her that coffee is a drug, but, as Mavis pointed out, coffee drinkers do not lock themselves in their rooms and never talk to their parents.

Actually, Don did love his folks. It was just that right now he was totally into his music. But they thought something was wrong. One Friday night, when Don and his band, Trash, were playing for a dance at the Armory, Earl and Mavis went in and shook down his room. Under the bed they found a box of tapes, numbered 1 through 4 and marked Songs. They played them and found out they were songs written and sung by Don. They were about subjects he had never discussed at home, such as anger and violence. One song was about going down the street and tripping up nuns, and although the Beemans were not Catholic, they were shocked.

The next morning, Earl spoke to Don. He didn't mention the songs, but he told Don to quit being moody around home and to make good use of his time, instead of hanging around with a bunch of punks who were up to no good. "We didn't bring you up to be just another dumb punk," Earl told him. "Sometimes you make me ashamed to be your parent."

Actually, punk rock, as it is called, has brought about some useful changes in popular music, as many respected rock critics have pointed out, and its roots can be traced back to the very origins of rock itself and perhaps even a little bit farther. "It goes without saying," Green Phillips has written in *Rip It Up: The Sound of the American Urban Experience*, "that punk rock is outrageous. Outrage is its object, its *raison d'être*, its very soul. It can also be said to be mean, filthy, stupid, self-destructive, and a menace to society. But that does not mean we should minimize its contribution or fail to see it for what it truly is: an attempt to reject the empty posturing of the pseudo-intellectual album-oriented Rock-as-Art consciousness cult of the post-*Pepper* era and to recreate the primal persona of the Rocker as Car Thief, Dropout, and Guy Who Beats Up Creeps."

Punk-rock bands, Phillips goes on to say, through their very outrageousness—the musicians spitting onstage, cursing and throwing things at the audience, breaking up dressing rooms, trying to burn down auditoriums, and sometimes seriously injuring their managers and road crews—have forced many critics to re-examine certain pre-punk assumptions, such as the role of criticism.

As it turned out, criticism was exactly what Earl gave Don, especially after the President's Day County 4-H Poultry Show dance, at which Trash played. Actually, the dance wasn't so bad. The band was rowdy and yelled a lot of tough, punk types of stuff at the audience, but that was their thing, after all, and nobody really minded until Trash's drummer, Bobby Thompson, spat at Sharon Farley while she was being crowned Poultry Show Queen on the stage between numbers. He said that she had given him a stuck-up look, but Mrs. Goodrich, the senior 4-H Club adviser, ordered him to leave the poultry barn instantly. But the kids thought it had been done just in fun, and yelled until she decided to let him stay, on condition that he didn't do any more of that sort of thing.

Of course, this was a direct challenge to the others in the band. Brian Bigelow, the bass player, spat at Mrs. Goodrich as she left the stage, and then, with the crowd yelling and egging them on, the others in the band made belching noises and lifted up their shirts. Don and the other guitarist, Art Johnson, turned their amps up full blast, and soon feed pellets were flying back and forth. Things were just about completely out of hand when suddenly a guy tossed a chicken on the stage and Bobby grabbed it and bit its neck.

Instantly, the barn was hushed. "Did you *see* that!" some people murmured. "See *what?*" other people whispered. Trash packed up their equipment quickly, while several exhibitors chased and then caught the chicken. Somebody took it to a vet. Everyone went home.

The next morning at breakfast, Earl picked up the *Gazette* and found his son on page 1. "4-H DANCE ENDS IN RIOT AS ROCK BAND EATS LIVE BIRD," the headline said. According to the story, police were investigating the incident, which one observer at the scene called "an act of bestiality reminiscent of Nazi Germany."

Earl, a veteran of the Second World War, exploded. He kicked open Don's bedroom door, flung himself at his son, who had only just awakened, and hauled him out of bed by one leg. "Why?" he screamed. "Why? Why? Why?" He swung wildly at the dumbfounded youth with the rolled-up newspaper.

"Why do you do everything possible to disgrace us?" he yelled. "Why must you search for ways to show your hatred and contempt? Even if you have no respect for us, do you have no respect for yourself? How can you do this? Is there no limit?"

"Dad," Don said when Earl finally paused for breath. "Dad, it's only music."

"It's only music," Earl repeated dumbly. "It's only music. You drag our name in the mud, and you say it's only music. I suppose the next thing you'll tell me is it's only a chicken!"

Actually, it *was* only a chicken, as Don and his friends kept telling each other when they met that night in Bobby's garage to rehearse. They hadn't shot a deer or gutted a fish or slaughtered a pig or thrown a lobster into a pot of boiling water. One of them, in the excitement of the moment, had simply bitten the neck of a chicken—a chicken that, as it turned out, was going to be perfectly O.K. They had the vet's word on that.

"They are trying to pin on us all the violence and hatred that are in their own hearts," said Brian, hanging up his big bass speaker on a rafter. "They think our music is violent just because it shows them where *they* are at and they don't dare to admit it."

"They can try all they want but they'll never stop rock and roll," Bobby said, referring to Mrs. Goodrich, who had already called up all of the county 4-H Club advisers, several youth ministers, a lot of high school teachers, and the county extension agent to arrange an emergency meeting that night.

"TEEN LEADERS VOW ANTI-ROCK DRIVE, AIM SMUT BAN IN AREA,"

the *Gazette* reported the following morning. "Longtime youth worker Diane Goodrich enjoys having a good time as much as the next person [the story went on], but Monday night, watching a local rock band rip into a live chicken with their teeth at the 4-H Poultry Show dance, she decided it was time to call 'foul.' Evidently, more than a few people agree with her. Last night, at a meeting in the high school auditorium attended on a word-of-mouth basis by literally dozens of parents, not to mention civic leaders and youth advisers, she spoke for the conscience of a community when she said, 'Have we become so tolerant of deviant behavior, so sympathetic toward the sick in our society, that, in the words of Bertram Follette, we have lost the capacity to say, This is not far out. You have simply gone too far. Now we say No!?' "

Don walked slowly home from school that day. A B+ student, he was sensitive to the accusations made against him and his friends, and while he knew that the uproar had been caused at least partly by irresponsible reporting in the media, he also realized that the time had come for both sides to cool their rhetoric and sit down and talk. In his mind, he sought ways for his dad and himself to resolve their differences, but he couldn't think of a single one. Actually, their relationship had been pretty good—at least, on a hunting-and-fishing level. Earl had taught Don how to handle a shotgun and tie a fly and clean a fish and take care of a skillet and, most of all, how to sit still all morning in the blind. Actually, that was a problem. In hunting and fishing, it is important, of course, to be absolutely quiet. Don and Earl had spent whole days on Stone Lake casting into rocky inlets for bass, and if Don so much as rattled an oarlock Earl glared at him. Don was never encouraged to share with his dad his feelings about himself or his hopes for the future. He was expected to sit and not scare fish.

It was a shaken Trash, an incensed Trash, that met in the Thompsons' garage after supper on Wednesday. "We're going to show them," Brian vowed, his fists clenched white, "that we can be everything they say we are. They tell lies about us—O.K., we're going to make those lies come true!"

That night, they played with wild abandon. The garage windows rattled as the band members blew off their frustration at having been attacked for something that had been blown up way out of proportion.

> Baby, you call me an animal for
> something I didn't do,
> Well, if that's how you want it
> I'm going to be wild for you!

At the word "wild," the boys lunged forward and crouched and grinned like madmen.

> Well, O.K., baby, you think you're
> Little Red Riding Hood,
> I'll be the Big Bad Wolf, and this
> time I'll get you good.

Here, Art stomped on the blitz pedal, throwing his amp into overdrive, while Don beat on his Ripley B-19 with windmill chops, and Brian actually straddled the bass and rode it like a horse. Bobby leaped from the drums and, with one yank, started up his father's lawn mower, to which they had taped a microphone.

> I'm gonna ride my mower all
> around this town

> Cut everybody who's been trying to
> put me down!

Now they moved into the finale. The lawn mower was stopped and the band fell silent, except for the *bump-bump-bump* of Brian's bass, as Bobby staggered forward like somebody completely out of his mind—panting, groping, and stumbling, with his eyes wild—while Brian sang:

> Well, you call us trash, so what
> do we have to lose?
> We're gonna be so bad you can
> read it in the morning news!

Suddenly Bobby leaped into the air, rushed forward, reached into a cardboard box, and grabbed a chicken and bit it again and again, until the feathers flew.

Actually, it was just a pillow they had put there for the rehearsal, but it seemed real to Trash, who sat back exhausted after the song. They all had experienced a tremendous release from it, and yet they were stunned at what had happened.

"Like I wasn't even aware of what I was doing," Bobby said. "I couldn't believe it was me. It was that great."

"It's bigger than us," Art said. "I get into it and I am just completely blown away."

"I don't know if we should actually ever do it," Don said. "If you think we really should, then I guess so, but I really don't know."

"I don't think we should do it unless we're really into it, but if it's going to happen, then I say let it happen," Brian said.

On Wednesday evening, Earl and Mavis were sitting in their forest-green lounger chairs beside the fireplace in the basement family room, reading the sports and family sections, respectively, of the *Gazette*. There was more about Mrs. Goodrich and her Committee for Teen Decency on the family page ("ROCK-RECORD ROAST SLATED FOR SUNDAY"), but by now Mavis was able to read articles on the subject without tears. "I don't know, I feel they are being unfair to Don and his friends," she said to Earl. "They are making a mountain out of what was probably just a joke. Mrs. Thompson told me that Bobby didn't even draw blood on that chicken. All it suffered was a slight neck sprain. She said that when Bobby was little he would tease his sister by pretending to eat angleworms. Maybe this is the same thing."

"Time they grew up, then," Earl said. "They walk around like they got the world on a string. Never listen to a thing you say. Treat you like dirt. Maybe this'll give them a taste of their own medicine."

"I don't know," Mavis said thoughtfully. "A mother doesn't have all the answers. Sometimes I'm upset by little things they do or say. Sometimes I wonder. But in the end I know he's still my boy. I may not always understand, but I know he needs me to be here, to listen, to forgive. And I know there's nobody so bad but what they deserve a second chance."

Earl and Mavis talked a long time that night. They remembered the many good times they had had with Don—the pleasure he had given them, the many wonderful memories. Mavis recalled that Don's first word had been Papa, and Earl recalled that his second was chicken. They both had a good laugh over that!

"They were good years, Mave," Earl said, his eyes glistening. "I've been wrong about Don. I'll do better now."

"Tomorrow is a new day," she replied brightly.

"He's a good boy if only we'd give him a chance," said Earl, practically weeping.

"Just like his daddy," said Mavis, reaching for his hand.

"Let's go up to bed," said Earl, rising. He held her tightly.

"I think this is just going to bring us closer together," she said.

Don couldn't sleep Wednesday night. He had gotten up twice, once to swipe a pack of his dad's Salems and then to get the blackberry wine left over from Christmas, and now, as he lay in bed drinking and smoking and carefully exhaling toward the fan that hummed in the window, he felt torn between his deep love of music and his fears that Trash was going off the deep end. He had confessed this doubt to Brian at school, and Brian said, "If it feels good, then what's wrong?" Don was not completely certain in his own mind if this made sense or not. How can you feel good if you don't know it's right, he wondered. And how do you know if something is right?

After talking to Brian, he had spent his lunch hour in the library, searching the short shelf marked Philosophy & Religion for a book that might clarify his thinking, and now he reached for it on the bedside table. It was *The Art of Decision-Making*, by M. Henry Fellows. A paragraph from the preface had impressed him, and now he read it again:

> In a society appearing often paralyzed by an overload of complex decisions, the act of decision-making may assume primary importance over the actual meaning and effect of the decision itself; or, to put it another way, a crucial function of the decision-making process is to assert the power to decide. It is necessary to make this point absolutely clear: in an increasingly complicated society, the act of making decisions is clearly not a matter of choice but a matter of necessity.

Once again Don knew he must decide whether to stay in Trash and risk banishment from home and the permanent hatred of a community (and perhaps a nation) united in outrage at the

senseless injury (or even death) of a barnyard fowl, or not, and
he had to decide before their next public appearance.

The next morning, Mavis got on the phone to the other Trash
parents, and that evening, in the Beeman living room, the eight
of them agreed that the boys had been treated unfairly and
deserved a second chance. "Let's put on a dance ourselves!" Art's
mom suggested, and everybody said, "Why not?" That week,
Earl arranged through his union to rent the Bricklayers Hall
for a low rate, and Mrs. Thompson, who worked for an ad
agency, formed her media friends into a publicity committee.
Mavis took charge of refreshments, and Mr. Thompson talked
the mayor, an old fishing buddy, into granting them a provi-
sional dance permit. "We'll have to move fast before the City
Council can rescind it," he said. "Saturday night's the night."

Trash rehearsed Thursday night in the Thompsons' garage.
Although they knew their folks had gotten behind them, they
didn't discuss the planned dance, now tentatively titled (Mrs.
Thompson's idea) A Salute to Youth. Perhaps they couldn't
believe it was true. Once again the music was so powerful, so
all-encompassing, that the boys got carried away and went right
into "They Call Us Trash." "Let's not do that song tonight,"
Don had asked, but they did—they couldn't help it—and they
played even more wildly than before, perhaps because of a strobe
light that Art had borrowed from his dad, a mechanic, who
used it for balancing wheels. The effect of the strobe was fright-
ening. Bobby ate practically half the pillow before they could
get it away from him. They had to sit on him and hold him
down, even though they were pretty shaky themselves. When
they had quieted down a little, they tried out Brian's new song,
which he had written that day:

> All my life you told me "Shut
>   up and behave."
> Well, from now on, Mama, your
>   boy's gonna scream and rave.

> I know you hate to see me playing
>   rock and roll,
> But Mom, I gotta break your
>   heart to save my soul.

Later on, Don would remember the last line as the point at which he had begun to make his decision.

Don came home from school Friday and, as usual, put on a record and fixed himself a peanut-butter-on-toast sandwich and a glass of milk. The phone rang just as the toast popped up. "Long distance calling for a Donald Beeman," said an operator's voice.

"This is him," Don answered.

"Go ahead," she said.

"Don," said a deep voice at the other end. "Green Phillips here, at *Falling Rocks*."

Falling Rocks! At the mention of the name of the country's leading rock tabloid, Don's mind went completely numb. *Falling Rocks!* But—

"Don, we have a photographer who is flying out there right now on a chartered jet to cover your concert tomorrow," Phillips went on. "I'll be doing the story from here, and I need something from you over the phone. I'm going upstairs in a minute and I'm going to try to sell this thing as a cover story, but at the moment I'm up against a Beatles-reunion rumor and a Phil Spector retrospective and God knows what else, so I need something to put us over the top. Don, I'm going to put it straight to you. I'm up against a bunch of editors who don't know what's going on, and I need to know something right now—not tonight, not tomorrow morning, not maybe, but yes or no. Is your guy going to eat the chicken or isn't he?"

"What did you tell him?" Bobby grabbed Don's shoulders and shook him and hugged him at the same time.

"I said probably."

"Probably?"

"I said yes, I was pretty sure, it looked like that was going to happen."

"It's in the *bank!*" Bobby yelled. "It's not *going* to happen. It's *happening!*"

"Geek Rock is a style that departs radically from the punk genre even as it transcends it," Green Phillips explained in the cover story he typed out that night. "It is music with a mythic urge, raw and dirty and yet soaring off into the cosmic carny spirit of primitivist America and the sawdust world of the freak show of the soul, starring Tamar, Half Girl and Half Gorilla, and Koko, the Wild Man from Borneo Who Eats Live Spiders.

"For all the macho leather and scarred brilliance of its Presleys, Vincents, or Coopers," he wrote, "rock has always stayed within the bounds of urban sensibility—a more ordered world that has filed rebellion and outrage into the thematic grid of heavy drinking, hard fighting, hot cars, and fast sex. The achievement of Trash is to take us, as punk rock never can, into the darkest backroads of the heartland, back into the sideshow tent of the American experience, and, inevitably, of course, back into ourselves."

On Saturday morning, Don slept late, and when he awoke he longed to go downstairs and plead with his mom and dad. "Please cancel A Salute to Youth. Don't ask why—just cancel it immediately," he wanted to tell them. But he knew it was too late for reappraisal. Whatever was going to happen had gained too much momentum.

The three hundred friends and relatives of Trash who jammed the Bricklayers Hall that night (including a number of ministers who believed that the basic message of rock was caring and sharing, as well as Don's grandma, who was hard of hearing) knew no such trepidation. They piled into the hall as if they were going to a party. It took Mr. Thompson, who was master of ceremonies, several minutes to get all the people to take their seats and give him their attention. He spoke briefly on the importance of trust in human relationships and then, to brighten the occasion with a little humor, he shouted, "And now, back *safe and sound* from its last engagement . . ." and waved toward the wings, and out came the treasurer of the 4-H Club bearing a chicken with a bandaged neck. He put it down in its cage at the front of the stage, and the crowd gave the chicken a standing ovation.

Trash leaped out onstage, ready to play for keeps. "We Come to Rock," "Look Out, Danger," "Electric Curtains," "It Hurts Me More," and "Dirty, Desperate, Born to Die" (all originals) led off the show and were appreciated by almost everyone. Many people in the crowd, including all the Trash parents, got up to dance to the crackling beat, which seemed to pound up through the floor. Some of the parents had learned this particular dance in adult-education classes. "They certainly do get quite a sound out of secondhand instruments!" Mrs. Thompson called to Mavis Beeman. Mavis was nervous. "Don't they look a little feverish to you?" she asked. Don had actually been feeling sick all day. His face was flushed and his stomach was upset, but he had refused to let his mother take his temperature. "Nothing at all," he said when she asked what was wrong. But later he came into the kitchen during supper and said maybe it would be better if she and Earl stayed home tonight, that it might be too late for them.

"Of course not," she had said. "We *want* to be there."

Now it was eleven o'clock—they had promised the Bricklayers to be through by eleven-thirty—and, standing at the back of the hall, trying to see over the dancers, Mavis was stricken by the sight of the chicken, still up there in its cage. She didn't know why, but she felt sure that if she could only reach the stage in time . . . "Stop the music!" she cried. She pushed forward into the waves and currents of bodies, which shoved and battered against her as the band sang, "You call me an animal for something I didn't do."

"Don, it's not too late!" she hollered, but it was, and her efforts only served to give her a front-row seat for a sight she would never forget the rest of her life: a brief moment of eye contact with a chicken as it fixed her with an expression of utter reproach in the split second before Bobby tore open the cage.

"Perhaps no bird, not even the eagle, bluebird, or robin, has entered so deeply the folk consciousness of the race as has the common chicken (*Gallus gallus*)," Green Phillips had written. "Indeed, throughout the Christian world, and even in many non-Christian countries, the chicken, from Plymouth Rock to lowly Leghorn, has come to stand for industry, patience, and fecundity, and, through its egg, for life itself, rebirth, and the resurrection of Christ, and, through its soup, for magical healing and restoration of the spirit. And yet, even as the chicken rides high as symbol of the Right Life in the pastoral dreams of the post-agrarian bourgeoisie, its name has attracted other connotations—of pettiness, timidity, and foolishness—perhaps reflecting our culture's doubts about itself. It is the peculiar genius of Trash to exploit this dichotomy to its fullest resolution, and thus to release in an audience such revulsion as can only indicate that profound depths have been reached."

Trash spent Saturday night at the Thompsons'. Mrs. Thompson had said that she would not speak to them but she would not turn them away, either, and they were welcome to sleep in the basement. Mr. Thompson was out consoling the Beemans, who had taken it hard, especially Mavis. Don called home Sunday afternoon, and his mom hung up on him.

Trash spent Sunday night on a bus to Omaha and put up at a Holiday Inn, and on Monday night played one set as an opening act to Sump, at the Armory. Advance ticket sales had been sluggish for weeks, until the promoter booked Trash on the strength of a page 2 photo in the Sunday paper showing Bobby with a faceful of feathers under the headline "CHICKEN SLAIN BY MIDWEST SINGER." Quickly reprinted on posters, it boosted box office some, but in the drafty hall, playing on borrowed gear to a strange and scattered audience, Trash couldn't work up to the emotional peak they needed to make the whole thing work. The new chicken sat in its cage and shivered, and when the time came Bobby hadn't the heart to do more than just pick it up and shake it. The crowd, which naturally expected more, booed them off the stage.

But actually it wasn't bad for starters. They got six hundred dollars for the night's work and a telephone call offering them a job in Tampa as opening act for the Ronnies, a successful band that already had an album, *Greatest Hits*, and was already popular in some places, including Wilkes-Barre, Gary, Erie, Louisville, and Baton Rouge. The Ronnies, who were into a combination of punk and heavy metal plus some middle of the road along with jazz, liked some of Trash's music O.K., but they were really turned on by the idea of the chicken bit. When they all met in Tampa to rehearse, the Ronnies cut Trash's set down to three songs and worked up a fifteen-minute routine for the chicken, with strobes and costumes and choreography and a truckload of chicken feathers to dump on the audience at the end. Bobby had to rehearse the chicken bit fourteen times that afternoon, but the Ronnies' manager, a little guy named Darrell Prince, was still not satisfied. Bobby sort of seemed to have lost interest in the whole idea. "I don't know," he said. "I really don't know."

That night, before Trash's first show with the Ronnies, Darrell Prince came up to Don in the dressing room. "You're doing the chicken," he said to him.

"I don't know," Don said. "To tell you the truth, I've never done it before."

"You watched the other kid do it. Just do what he did."

"Well, to be perfectly honest with you, it's not actually something that I am particularly into right now."

"*Get* into it," the guy said, and he talked to Don for several minutes about rock and roll as a ritual expression of tribal unity which sets free powerful feelings, including anger and guilt, that require a blood sacrifice to restore the inner peace and harmony of the tribe. He gave examples of this from Mayan and early Japanese cultures, the Old Testament, NFL Sunday football, and the Spanish bullring. "Besides," he said, "it's only a chicken."

"I don't know," Don said. "I honestly don't think I could do it that *well*. People pay four, five dollars to get in, they deserve to see a good show. I might just get sick, or something."

But Darrell Prince walked away, and a few minutes later Don and the rest of his friends were standing in a corridor of the amphitheatre ready to go on, and there was another chicken in a cage, and they could all hear the sounds of the crowd, which was already whistling and clapping for them to come out. Don did feel sick, and he didn't know if he was going to be able to do it or not. While he waited, he thought to himself that perhaps by doing it and feeling sick about doing it he would do some good, perhaps by showing any kids that might be in the audience that they should not try to do this, and that maybe it would be an example to them about violence. And besides, that afternoon the *Falling Rocks* story had come out, and they were some sort of stars.

WLT (THE EDGAR ERA)

It was their sandwiches and their magnificent sandwich palace on Nicollet Avenue, not radio broadcasting, that brought the Elmore brothers, Edgar and Roy, to wealth and prominence in Minneapolis. In 1919, a few years before electric refrigerators were common, the brothers sold their ice company at a fine profit, purchased the former Sons of Knute Temple, and opened Elmore's Court restaurant, with six sandwiches on the menu: egg salad, onion and cucumber, toasted cheese, ham, ham and cheese, and the Hamburg. All were delicious, but the egg salad was tops. Three inches thick at the middle and served on wheat bread with a hard crust, the Elmore egg salad was a Minneapolis landmark, a lunch beloved by thousands, and, because the sandwich craze was then sweeping the Midwest, a gold mine for Edgar and Roy. Among the better families, however, the sandwich was still scorned as an inferior food, served free in taverns and eaten by mechanics, and so they did not patronize the Court. Roy, who managed the kitchen and who was something of a freethinker, didn't give a darn for them, the Peaveys and the Heffelfingers and the Pillsburys—all cake-eaters, to him—but it was Edgar's weakness to covet their patronage, and once the Court was on its feet he set out to improve its quality and tone.

Edgar was a fine old gentleman, a devout Presbyterian and a natty dresser (red polka-dot tie with a navy-blue suit, navy-blue bow tie with a white linen suit), and in the majesty of the Court—with its oak tables beneath a blue-and-gold stained-glass skylight, its neo-Norwegian columns supporting the marble mezzanine, and, upstairs, its walnut-paneled Throne Room with oil portraits of Past Knutes and their lovely Elses—Edgar was more the admiral than a sandwich-palace proprietor. His glance could straighten a man in his chair and quicken the step of a waiter, but in matters of improving quality and tone, he was nervous, indirect, and uncertain.

He invested in a string quartet to play at lunchtime—Schubert mostly, and some Mozart and Beethoven (the slow movements)—but he wasn't sure he liked the music, so he hid the musicians in a forest of ferns. He labored at writing advertisements extolling the beauties of the Court, its music, its architecture, its civility ("The establishment to which gentlemen repair with no fear of embarrassment"). "People will take us for a French whorehouse," said Roy, for Edgar never wrote a word about *sandwiches*. The radio station was Roy's idea. Radio, Roy said, would take Elmore's right *to* the Pillsburys in their own homes; they could hear for themselves what a fine place it was. (Also, it would give Roy Jr. something to do with himself; he was unhappy in his job as egg buyer, and he talked of nothing but radio.)

Edgar was sixty-two. He had misgivings about assuming a new headache like a radio station at his age. He worried about the expense, the danger of electrocution, and the possible influence of radio waves on the mental processes, but he also saw the Pillsburys seated around a radio receiver in their mansion, enjoying the fine music from Elmore's Court. And so on April 6, 1925, patrons came to lunch to find the Throne Room draped with velvet, the tables arranged in a semicircle, and in the center a bastion of broad-leafed plants from which rose a black iron stand adorned with a golden eagle, the Stars and Stripes, and a microphone.

Of the six sandwiches, the one most in need of association with fine music was the Hamburg, which many people still shunned out of leftover patriotism, and it was this sandwich, a simple beef patty in a bun, that Station WLT (With Lettuce and Tomato) was intended particularly to assist. The first broadcast featured the Hamburg Tuxedo Trio (formerly the Three Nicolleteons) and Miss Lily Dale, the Hamburg Soprano, who sang that day—and every day thereafter for eight years—the Hamburg Song (to the tune of "Over There"): "It's the one, it's the one, it's the one with the fun in the bun. When you eat a Hamburg, you always clamor for just another one, one, one." Dedication Day also included two spirituals and an original song, "The Laughing Water of Minnehaha," by the Trio, and selections by Schubert, Mozart, and Beethoven, played by the Court Orchestra (the string quartet plus a piano). Finally, Edgar was brought up for a few words. He set his feet firmly, grasped the microphone with both hands, pressed it to his lips, and prayed in a loud voice that all of this might turn out for the best and be found pleasing in the eyes of God. His prayer practically deafened Roy Jr., who was at the controls in the linen closet, but, all in all, everyone judged the day a complete success. After the broadcast, there was a reception.

Oh the days when radio was strange and dazzling! Even the WLT performers could not quite believe it. To think that their voices flew out as far as Anoka, Stillwater, and Hastings! And yet it seemed to be true. Roy Jr. had friends in those towns who had promised to listen, and they said WLT came in loud and clear, so the proof was there, but some didn't accept it for years—not entirely. For years, Clarence Peters, the Tuxedo tenor, would remark to his wife in the evening about a particularly good number he had sung on the radio that day, "You should have heard it!" "I *did* hear it, as clear as a bell," she always would say. Of course, Clarence knew this, and yet, never having heard it himself, he wasn't ready to believe it.

One day, unable to bear the mystery, Clarence backed away from the microphone during the last chorus of "Cowboy's Farewell," edged toward the door to the linen closet, opened it, and, still singing ("I am gone away to a home in the sky, where love never fades and hopes never die"), recognized his own voice on the receiving set nearby, and cried out, "I have heard it!" Sensing immediately that the home audience might not grasp the meaning of his remark, he quickly added, "I am on the radio!"

Because of his good enunciation and presence of mind, Clarence Peters soon became WLT's first announcer, and as such he performed the first broadcast interview in Minnesota. Miss Dale was ill that day, the Trio was strapped for new songs, and Clarence, needing to fill a few minutes, took the microphone to the nearest table and invited those present to make a talk. A tall man in a white suit (his name has been forgotten) stood up and nervously donned his straw hat as the microphone was put before him. "It is an honor to be given this opportunity," he said gravely, "and I sincerely thank you for it."

This speech, though brief, was a real innovation at the time—

the voice of an ordinary person, a person such as the listener himself or herself, carried to countless unseen homes, the same as if he or she were the Governor, or the Archbishop, or a Pillsbury—and soon the whole city knew that Elmore's was the place to go to "get on the air." Hundreds vied for the choice tables in the Throne Room; families from distant towns journeyed to Minneapolis to visit Elmore's, having alerted neighbors and friends to listen to their broadcast. Many were prepared to pay money for the privilege. Some demanded it as a right. Edgar had to hire two ushers to handle the crowds. The Throne Room became a regular auditorium—people were too excited to eat anyway, even with the ushers to shush them—so the tables were hauled downstairs to the main dining room and replaced by pews from the Knute chapel.

It was wonderful to be on the radio, and awful. Many a man who had rehearsed words in his mind found himself tongue-tied at the crucial moment, and sat down in shame and wept. Many a man who had thought to tell a joke chucked it at the last moment in favor of a religious or patriotic sentiment befitting the importance of the occasion. ("This is Albert M., of Waseca. Hello. For all have sinned and come short of the glory of God.") Some requested prayers for sick friends. Respect for the flag was expressed, and the need for vigilance; also the superiority of Minnesota cheese and butter, the beauty of her lakes and rivers, the belief in democracy, the hope for a better future.

Through that first summer and winter and into the next summer, Edgar pondered what he had wrought—the once lovely restaurant now crowded and noisy, waiters quitting every week, and, thanks to WLT, the Hamburg now the hot item on the menu. This was a bitter pill for Roy and the cooks, Dorothy and Inga, who resented the hard assembly-line work of frying Hamburgs by the hundreds, and got sick from the grease. What was worse, Edgar had to contend with hundreds of patrons who demanded radio time and old regulars who expected special consideration, and soon he was hounded by musicians, singers, actors, poets, comedians, and entertainers of every stripe, who saw radio as their chance to be presented at last to the Minnesota audience. These included some good ones who later became famous: Whistling Jim Wheeler and His All-Boy Band, Elsie and Johnny, "Ice Cream" Cohen, Norma Neilsen and Fargo Bill, the Orphan Girls Quartet, and many more. But most of them were the others—the child elocutionists, yodelers, mandolin bands, gospel-singing families, people who did barnyard sounds and train imitations, and dozens of Autoharp players, all of whom had to be refused, some of them repeatedly. "We have opened a Pandora's box," Edgar said, "and now everyone and his brother is trying to get into it."

At first, Edgar was puzzled by the performers' ambition, and then, as he brooded on it, he became wary, and at last a fear took hold of him that never let go for the rest of his life. He decided that, while most people were harmless, some ("and it only takes one") were not. He imagined that they were driven by a desire to ruin him by doing something awful on his radio station—a vulgar remark shouted by a stranger in the audience, an off-color story, perhaps filth in a foreign language. He saw someone latching on to the microphone, wresting it away from Clarence, and saying *something*—something so repulsive, crude, and vile as to make his name Mud in thousands of homes, including the Pillsburys'. They would never be seen in a place where things like that were allowed. "We are helpless," he told Roy. "We work ourselves sick to make a good restaurant, and now the kitchen is a hellhole, and the sandwiches I wouldn't feed to a dog, and now anyone who wants to could walk in and put us out of business in a minute."

Edgar swung into action. He hired a young English teacher,

Miss Phelps, to observe the audience for any who appeared agitated. The public-speaking time was limited strictly to fifteen minutes in the morning and a half hour in the afternoon, and Roy Jr. was instructed to keep a hand on the switch at those periods and be ready to throw it instantly. Edgar hired two announcers, big sturdy fellows, and showed them how to keep both feet planted during interviews and how to place one hand on the person's shoulder so as to have good leverage if push came to shove. He wrote up a WLT code covering all aspects of broadcasting ("The Principles of Radiation"), and he made all performers agree to it. It included a dress code, "Subjects To Be Avoided," and "Regulations Concerning Music." "By the grace of God, it is given to us to cast our bread on distant waters," he wrote in the code. " 'See then that ye walk circumspectly, not as fools, but as wise.' Eph. 5:15." And he drew up a program schedule and ordered that it be followed, no exceptions:

10:30 *Piano Prelude*
10:45 *The Homemakers Hour*
11:00 *Morning Musicale*
11:45 *Meet Your Neighbors*
12:00 *Let's Sing!*
12:30 *Orchestral Interlude*
12:45 *The Hamburg Tuxedo Trio Hour*
 1:00 *Let's Get Together*
 1:30 *Orchestral Interlude*
 1:45 *Scripture Nugget*
 2:05 *Miss Lily Dale*
 2:20 *Up in a Balloon*
 2:35 *The Classroom of the Air*
 3:00 *Obituaries and Notices*
 3:10 *The Story Hour*
 3:25 *Piano Postlude*

Gone forever were the days when Clarence might reminisce about his Wisconsin boyhood for ten minutes until the missing sheet music was found, or the Trio repeat the verses of "The Lost Chord," or Evelyn Wills Duvalier carry on endless impromptu piano variations because nobody knew what was supposed to happen next, or when a person in the audience might rise to give a demonstration of cow-calling.

As WLT neared the end of its first decade, Edgar turned over the management to Roy Jr. He was tired of listening to the radio for five hours every day and worrying that someone (the same old *someone*, who hadn't turned up yet but was only prolonging the suspense) would go over the edge and give him a good solid heart attack. He didn't care much for WLT. The Trio mumbled words, and Miss Lily Dale sounded like a goat, and nobody sang the songs that he wanted to hear. And it was more tiresome to listen now that he was getting hard of hearing. Roy Jr. had built him a receiver so powerful that it rattled windows, and another one was installed in his Buick (the first car radio in Minneapolis) which could be heard for blocks. People complained to the police. Edgar was always switching the darned thing off, but he was uneasy with it off, and he was always turning it back on. To give him a rest, Roy Jr. scheduled a fifteen-minute newscast at one o'clock, Edgar's naptime; Edgar appreciated the gesture, but every day he expected *someone* to put in an appearance.

One show that always lifted his spirits (and that he himself sponsored) was "Up in a Balloon," with Vince Upton and his wife, Sheridan Thomas, playing the parts of Bud and Bessie, a wealthy Minneapolis couple who roam the earth in a luxurious balloon, seeking adventure. Edgar loved the show less for the dialogue, which was quite ordinary, than for the sound effects that Vince spent days and weeks perfecting. The balloon format was well suited to Vince's perfectionism for it allowed the couple to spend long periods in the stratosphere, which required only the creaking of the gondola (a horse halter) and the sighing wind (one of the Tuxedo Trio, or anyone handy), along with a spoken description of the scenery below, while Vince planned the effects for their next descent. WLT's modest budget did not permit the balloon to visit cities (there weren't enough staff members on hand to provide hubbub), and so its descents tended to be emergency landings in isolated regions. Even at that, Bud and Bessie crashed several times in the Arctic Circle before Vince was satisfied with his glacier effect, which was first an aluminum cookie tin (plied by Clarence) and then a bag of rock salt that was put through a meat grinder; finally, he hit on the idea of rolling a basketball containing a microphone along a bed of gravel. Likewise, he experimented for weeks to produce dripping rain on the leaves of a tropical forest, the shifting sands of the Sahara, and the pounding surf at Waikiki (fifty pounds of oats and a wheelbarrow).

Hundreds of new effects were subsequently created, many of them submitted by listeners, who strove to surpass each other with stranger and more exotic adventures: a wave of molten lava destroying a grain elevator, an army marching across thin ice, Bud and Bessie climbing the Eiffel Tower using suction cups, and (Edgar's invention) Bud and Bessie throwing their radio into the Grand Canyon during a broadcast of *Carmen* (the Court Orchestra seated on a freight cart, a portable tile wall, and an alarm clock). It was the invention of a disillusioned man with a great deal of leisure time.

The Depression years, in fact, were unhappy ones for Edgar. His doctors ordered him to stay away from the Court and to avoid those WLT programs that made him anxious (he was more anxious, though, when he couldn't hear them). Denied even the egg salad sandwich, his favorite, he took to his bed in the big house on Lake Calhoun, and sulked at nurses. Once, he tried to return the WLT license to the government, and, failing at that, changed his will to make the Pillsbury Company his beneficiary. He was not, as Roy Jr. later proved in court, a man of sound mind.

On October 12, 1940, his birthday, Edgar lay in bed and listened to "A Salute to Edgar Elmore" on WLT—all five hours of it. Beginning with "Piano Prelude," all of the music programs featured his favorite songs, and Lucille Larson gave the original egg salad recipe on "The Homemakers Hour." The neighbors on "Meet Your Neighbors" were his friends; the "Scripture Nugget," read by the Reverend Irving James Knox, was Edgar's beloved I Corinthians 10; the story on "The Story Hour" was his own life story. But the highlight surely was "Up in a Balloon," for Vince had gone all out. The episode, entitled "Bud and Bessie Visit the Old Testament," included the Creation, the destruction of Sodom and Gomorrah, and the parting of the Red Sea (ten quarts of motor oil and an upright vacuum cleaner).

The five hours were an eternity to Edgar. He was positive that *someone* had chosen this day, his day, to pull a fast one. As the last notes of "Piano Postlude" died out ("Lead, Kindly Light"), he turned to Roy and said, "I can't go through this again." He passed away exactly one month later.

The dread event that Edgar had waited fifteen years for occurred finally on August 7, 1942. It happened to Vince Upton during "The Story Hour." On that day, Vince, as "Grandpa Sam," sat down in "the old easy chair," invited his young listeners to gather close round their radios, and picked up the script and began to read. It didn't take him long to realize that *someone* had slipped him a wrong story, a story that began, "I was born twenty-seven years ago in a place called Northfield, Minnesota, the dullest little burg in the dullest state in the Union, and as soon as I was old enough to earn the train fare, I set out to see what life was all about."

Vince swallowed hard and continued. The story was the "confession" of a young man named Frank who gains wealth in Chicago and takes up with a dark Paraguayan beauty named Pabletta, whose breasts are pale and small and shiver at the thrill of his touch. Slowly, his voice shaking with the effort, Vince picked his way through the story, glancing ahead as he read and skirting the obvious outrages, but some things escaped his eye until he was right on top of them. These he read quickly, adding, "Of course, I knew I should not have done this," or "Something told me that someday I would be punished." The writer of the story had certainly tied it together tightly—you had to give him credit for that.

Finally, with ten minutes left, Vince arrived at an episode that seemed to lead the story in a direction that could not be pursued any further. Now Vince was a script man through and through and hated to speak impromptu, but he put the story aside and rose to the occasion. In a sad and weary voice, he confessed his sinful pride and sensual nature and begged the forgiveness of his family. He denounced the evil influence of movies and modern novels. He announced that the beautiful Pabletta had died beneath the wheels of a truck. "Today, doctors tell me that I have but weeks to live, my body ravaged by a disease without a name," he added, and concluded with an appeal to all within the sound of his voice to consider prayerfully what would be the outcome of their ways. "Repent! Repent!" he cried, and collapsed in tears just as the sweep hand approached twelve. "That's all for today. Be sure to join Grandpa Sam tomorrow at the same time for another exciting story," the announcer said, and Evelyn Wills Duvalier played "Just As I Am" from memory for "Piano Postlude."

After that, the scripts were guarded closely by Miss Phelps, who kept them hidden on her person and read and reread each one at the last moment before broadcast. As an extra precaution for his own peace of mind, Vince wrote an emergency "Story Hour" script, which he kept in an inside coat pocket and could switch to at any point, and which began, "But enough about that. Let's get on to today's main story, which concerns a young boy named Jim and his dog, Buster." This script, never used, lies today, yellow and stained, in the back of the loose-leaf copybook in the main WLT studio. Two generations of WLT announcers have revised the story in their spare time, polishing the dialogue, fleshing out the plot, introducing new characters, including Pabletta and her friend Ramón, and it is said to be quite good—though not, of course, suitable for broadcast.

THE SLIM GRAVES SHOW

Last summer, when Wingo Beals and His Blue Movers lost their 5:00 A.M. SunRise Waffle radio show because Wingo succumbed to the lure of the open road, I intended to complain to the sponsor because I had liked them so much. You'd think at least SunRise would have let the Movers (a fine band) have a *crack* at it on their own, but first I decided to give the new show a chance.

It was "The Slim Graves Show," and, like all the previous 5:00 A.M. SunRise shows (six in the last two years), consisted of the weather and livestock reports, letters from listeners, and about four songs—in their case, a solo by Slim or his wife, Billie Ann Twyman, a duet, an instrumental selection, and a hymn.

Soon I had to admit that Slim and his band, the Southland Sheikhs, were the best in every way. Though Slim's bass fiddle

was featured too often, in my opinion, the band was excellent—
especially the lead guitarist, Courteous Carl Harper the Guitar
Man. When he played "Orange Blossom Special" or "Dill Pickle
Rag" or any other difficult number, he really tore it apart, you
couldn't believe it was one person. Slim and Billie Ann were
extremely good vocalists, and there was enough talk so you got
to know the people personally. "You are my favorite band at
present and I look forward to hearing your show every morning,"
I wrote to them. "Keep up the good work. P.S. This is the
first fan letter I ever wrote."

Slim opened the show each day by whistling "Only a Pal."
Then he'd say something like this: "Good morning, friends and
neighbors, it's time for SLIM GRAVES and the Southland Sheikhs
for SUNRISE WAFFLES—gosh, they're good!—with more of that
good old-time music, so rise and shine, sit up and howl, there's
DAYLIGHT IN THE SWAMPS!" and the band would swing into
"The Slim Graves Special."

All went well for a few weeks and it seemed nothing could
stop them, but of course human nature will always take over
in the end, and underneath the great music there soon was
plenty of heartbreak for everyone. At first, you began to notice
how Billie Ann was getting down on Slim and making remarks
about him. She called him "Old Horseface—hope there aren't
any horses listening," and said he was hewed from native timber
but the ax slipped.

A little photo of them was on the SunRise box. Billie Ann
was fairly young and good-looking, though fat. Slim was perhaps fifty or fifty-five years of age and looked like he'd been in
a bad accident and not been sewn up right; his face was kind
of shoved together. The handsomest one (of course) was Courteous Carl, and of course Billie Ann fell for him like a box of
rocks. She and Slim had been on the road so long, now at last
they had a little cabin home, but she couldn't settle down. I

remember a song of hers called "Don't Be a Dog in My Manger," in which she made it quite clear she could have more fun without him, which wasn't surprising seeing as "His Whiskey's 90 Proof and His Love's 15."

OCTOBER 29: Surprise. Courteous Carl sings (not bad, either). Today he sang, "Let's be friends and forget about the past—something something last—there's nothing you can do, she walked away from you—something something—forgive me for I know she's yours but loyalty don't open many doors, and though we know marriage is made above we're not ashamed to be in love."

So it was out in the open in plain sight. Naturally, the listeners wrote in their comments, and in the following days Slim read all the letters on the air, even when it meant squeezing out the hymn. "Can't you see Billie Ann is trying to tell you to pay more attention to her and show her your love?" a woman wrote. "I know that if you do she'll come back fast. This happened to me and my husband about four years ago." But others threatened Billie Ann (and Carl) with personal harm. One woman said she'd tear Billie Ann's hair out if she got the chance.

Though Slim didn't say much, he made it plain to Billie Ann that he knew she was cheating on him. In one song, he named them by name and said, "She only pretended to love me and Carl'll never be happy because he'll always wonder if Billie Ann'll walk out on him just as she did to old Slim." Then he sang, "She cut up my heart with a knife and took the joy from out my life, She Gets Pleasure from Seeing Me Cry."

It seemed like Carl renewed his pledge of love to Billie every morning now, replacing Slim in the big duet spot, but while Billie sang with Carl, she was still in the SunRise commercials with Slim, fixing the golden-brown waffles for him as if nothing was wrong with their marriage. You just knew it couldn't go on.

Finally, around Christmastime, blood began to tell. Christmas made Billie Ann remember her childhood home and the promise she'd made to her folks to be more like Jesus every day. She certainly wasn't getting any closer this way. She spent Christmas Day in a bus depot holding a ticket to her home town of Tularemo, Arkansas. "I heard them call departure from Gate 3," she recalled, "but I was blinded by the tears of misery."

Slim kept at Billie, reminding her of what had been theirs, the hopes and dreams they'd shared, and the vows they'd made in that little country church so long ago. And their little daughter, in her innocent way, drove the message home in "A-D-U-L-T-E-R-Y (Don't Say That Word, It Makes Me Cry)." One morning, she asked her mother, "What is that word that begins with 'A' that Daddy said to you?" "It's a word, LaVerne, that big folks say that means I've been untrue," Billie Ann replied, weeping.

She was tormented, you could hear it in her voice. She loved Carl but you knew she was drawn to Slim and, in that part of her that needed someone to look after her, couldn't live without him. Carl was bright lights, liquor, and loud music. Slim was home. And yet she did love Carl and the way he made her feel good. But Carl has loved others and, like her, is of the wandering kind. Slim has only her, he's said more than once he'll always be true to her. Though, of course, Carl has, too.

JANUARY 10: In desperation, Billie Ann Twyman asks the radio audience to decide which man is right for her. We are to buy a box of SunRise Waffle Mix with the picture of the man we favor on the flap.

JANUARY 12: After giving it much thought, I have bought a Courteous Carl box. My reasons are as follows: While I admire Slim, I feel that Carl is a better man for her. He is going places and can advance her career in addition to making her happy.

Secondly, I don't believe she can return to Slim and have things be the same as before. Three, people do change and we should learn to accept it. According to the grocer, I am by no means in the minority. People are quietly buying up the Carl waffles. He tells how a man'll come in and buy one for old Slim and make a big speech about it, and later his wife'll come in and get ten or twelve for Carl.

JANUARY 17: Today Billie Ann was going to announce the results. Billie Ann: "First of all, I want to tell you how much I appreciate your letters and your prayers at this difficult time and your interest as shown in the number of people who have taken the opportunity to vote. I have never felt so torn before. I know I have done wrong and can never make it up to Slim, and yet my love for Carl is deep and sincere and has been very rewarding. I feel I owe it to myself, and to you, to give us another week in which to think about it."

Carl: "Just want to thank all who voted for me and urge you to get your friends to vote. Thanks again."

Slim: "I know there are thousands of you who feel as I do that nothing is more sacred than the bonds between man and wife. Now is your chance to speak up and say so. If you will only take this opportunity in the remaining week, I know we will come out on top."

JANUARY 24: A difficult week is over. I have purchased four boxes for Carl (including the one previous) and three for Slim. I find I am leaning more toward Slim the longer I think about it. I guess Billie Ann is, too. "You can't make a decision in two weeks whether or not to walk out on fifteen years of marriage," she says. The contest is extended.

JANUARY 25: Two women came to the door selling waffle boxes for Slim. I bought four. Later I went to the corner and bought

two more. I agree with Slim: "It's good to take more time
making up our mind. Too often we will act when passion's hot
to do what time will tell us we should not."

FEBRUARY 1: It's Slim for good: 10,451 to 7,285. Slim knew
she'd come back and holds no grudges. Billie Ann is giving up
her career for him. Slim is quitting the music business, too;
he'll go into life insurance for Fidelity Trust. But he has talked
SunRise into sponsoring Carl Harper on his own show.

So now it's "Courteous Carl Harper with the Pierce Sisters
and the Riders of the Sky for SunRise Waffles." The Pierce
Sisters, whose big hit was "A Big Brass Bed, a Rocker, and a
Range," are a very fine vocal ensemble. The instrumental number has been dropped, allowing the Sisters a spot for their talent.
Then, too, each of them gets her chance to do a duet with Carl.
Though it seems that the duet assignment goes more and more
often to one of the twins, Sharon and Sherrill Pierce, identical
sixteen-year-old beauties according to Carl, who is on the move
again. "I'm in trouble, seeing double, I feel like my head's in
a spin. Last night I kissed her (or was it her sister?). I don't
know where to begin," he says in "How Can I Give You My
Heart (If I Can't Even Tell You Apart)?" but it's pretty clear
he has his eye on both of them and you would think they could
see it but they go on hoping for the best and not realizing that
big trouble lies ahead.

FRIENDLY NEIGHBOR

Last year, forty-three from the Chaffee (N.D.) area traveled to
Freeport (Minn.) for the annual Dad Benson Friendship Dinner.
This year, thirty-eight of us from Freeport and New Munich
rode the bus up to Chaffee. The cost was twenty-five dollars
round trip (incl. dinner).

The Friendship Dinner, which is hosted by Chaffee in odd
years and Freeport in even, honors the memory of my uncle,
Walter "Dad" Benson, long beloved in the Midwest for his
"Friendly Neighbor" show from radio station WLT in Minneapolis. Uncle Dad, as we sometimes called him, was born in
Chaffee in 1894 and resided there for twenty-one years. After
his retirement in 1959 he removed to Freeport, where he lived
with me and Florence until 1965 when he passed away.

Once again the Freeport Association, of which I have the
pleasure to be president, sponsored a Hospitality Stop en route

in Fergus Falls for breakfast and refreshments. The stop was held at Fergus Implement, which carries our company's (Freeport Machine) line of creamers and automatic milking systems, both the 6-8's and the extendables. Dad Benson was closely associated with the company from 1953 to 1965. The winners of the two free trips to Chaffee and twenty-five-dollar bonds, Vi and Henry O'Connell, both members of the F.M. Twenty Year Employees Club, were also honored by myself, Brother Bob (vice-president), and Florence (treasurer).

The theme of the dinner was friendship and cooperation between Minnesota and North Dakota. It was emphasized that the two states share a common heritage of Christian culture. As the visiting delegation traditionally provides the speaker, the talk was given by Rev. Ernest Weiss of Freeport. Music was provided by Mr. and Mrs. N. P. Gruenewald, also of Freeport.

Walter "Dad" Benson was a nationally known personality from the days when "Friendly Neighbor" was carried by the Mutual Network, but the Midwest was always his home. He knew every small town and crossroads from his early years as a traveling seed-salesman, and they knew him as Dad. The show began at noon and in many areas the noon whistle was blown at 11:59 so that residents would have time to let their radios warm up. This was the case in Freeport. Everyone went directly to a radio and no business was done for twenty minutes. We heard the WLT chimes strike twelve, the organ play Dad's theme ("Whispering Lilacs"), and the announcer's voice say, "And now we take you down the road a ways to the home of Dad Benson, his daughter, Jo, and her husband, Frank, for a visit with the Friendly Neighbor, brought to you by Midland Fire & Casualty Insurance. As we join them, the family is sitting in the kitchen around the table where Jo is fixing lunch. . . ."

To those too young to remember the show, it probably seems corny, but to listeners the Bensons were as real as if they did live next door. Reverend Weiss recalled, "I once said to Dad, 'You were a pastor of the flock as much as I, or perhaps more so, for your sermons were in the form of stories, as the parables of old, and brought home spiritual truths far better than preaching ever could. Tens of thousands listened and tens of thousands responded to the message of love for one's fellow-man that was ever the keynote of "Friendly Neighbor." ' "

The roles of Frank and Jo were played for many years by Ed and Evelyn Moore, who now reside in Fargo and so were able to attend the dinner. Ed recalled how whenever the Benson family suffered a misfortune on the air, contributions would pour in to WLT. Of course the money was turned over to charity. "Dad's favorite charity was the Gilead Rest Home in Freeport," Ed told us, "and whenever the Home was short of funds, you could be sure Dad would work in some sort of crisis—a sudden hailstorm that wiped out the corn, a needed operation for the dog—and the deficit would be met. Once, for the Home's clothing drive, Dad went walking in his Sunday best and got sprayed by a skunk and I believe we received more than thirty good suits the next week."

But mostly Dad and Jo and Frank sat in the large kitchen around the table (now in the Midland employees' cafeteria). Every day Jo fixed lunch, soup and sandwiches or leftovers, and Dad would offer a poem or tell a story. Frank would read the grain futures and livestock market reports from the *Main Street Observer* and Jo would play the organ for the noontime hymn. The organist was Virginia Miles, now Mrs. N. P. Gruenewald.

From time to time on the show, the Bensons would listen to another radio show called "The Muellers." This show, of course, was imaginary. It was done in the adjoining studio by several actors and piped into the big studio where "Friendly

Neighbor" originated. The background of this is quite interesting. Every week, Dad received hundreds of letters from people with problems asking for his advice. He would select one letter and have the actors dramatize it on their "show." Then, while listening to it on his show, Dad would comment on what he thought the "Muellers" should do. In this way, he avoided any possible embarrassment to the letter writer.

For example, the Muellers might have a bad argument over money, and Dad would talk about money and how we never know what to do with what we have before we start wanting more. Or the Muellers might gossip about their friends, and Dad would "switch off" the "radio" and say that if you can't speak well of people not to say anything.

Shortly before Christmas Day, 1958, Dad received a letter from a little girl about her father. It moved Dad very deeply. And so, on Christmas, the Bensons tuned in "The Muellers" to hear the Mueller children crying because their father was not home. Mr. Mueller, it soon turned out, was involved with another woman and was spending Christmas at her house. Dad indicated his disapproval of this arrangement, but nevertheless it was very shocking to many listeners, who felt the show was too explicit (nowadays, of course, it would be considered tame by comparison). Hundreds of letters were received saying that the show had upset young children. Some ministers wrote in to say Dad should have taken a much stronger stand against the Muellers by not listening to their show at all. The philosophy of the Muellers was well known by this time, they said, and Dad's tolerating it in his own home could only set a poor example for other Christians. Of course, the dramatization had been entirely in the hands of the actors, but Dad accepted complete responsibility. On New Year's Day, "Friendly Neighbor" left the air.

After retirement, Dad seldom spoke about his radio days. He

would rather talk about his North Dakota boyhood, the good times and the hard times, and tell stories about farm life at the turn of the century. Every winter, he told the story about the Three-Day Blizzard of 1905 and how he got lost after breakfast trying to get to the barn not more than fifty yards away and spent a day and a night out on the open prairie until the storm broke. "Everywhere it was so white it hurt your eyes and you couldn't tell the difference between up and down if it weren't for your feet being so cold," Dad said. Dad often told this story on his many tours in behalf of the Freeport creamer, reminding his audience that the creamer can be switched on from the home. "If I'd a had one," he said, "I could've turned it on and followed the sound of it right to the milkhouse and from there to the barn."

In those days, when Dad was living with us in Freeport, people in Minnesota tended to make fun of North Dakotans and look down on them. If a person hailed from the Flickertail State, he was regarded as a hick. Of course, nobody felt this way about Dad and so he took it on himself to improve relations. It was his fondest wish that his Freeport neighbors should get to know his old friends from Chaffee, and it was the happiest day in his life when the first Friendship Dinner was held in Freeport in 1963 (there was no dinner in 1964, but then Chaffee hosted the 1965 affair, establishing the present even-odd rotation). Fourteen Chaffee residents were in attendance that day, and Dad was the guest of honor.

The Friendship Dinner is believed to be the only dinner of its type in the United States. Of course, it is not only a meal but a full day of activities. This year, we toured the Chaffee grain elevator and school and observed baling operations at a nearby farm, and there were horseshoe, checkers, and free-throw shooting tournaments, tractor rides, door prizes, a softball game, plus the dinner and evening sing. There was also a booth where collectors could swap tapes of Dad's shows. Of the more than 6,000 "Friendly Neighbor" shows that Dad did, we know of only 387 on tape. Among those that we've not located is the Christmas show of 1958. If anyone knows the whereabouts of that show, they should contact us in care of Freeport Machine.

THE TIP-TOP CLUB

The idea of pouring warm soapy water into overshoes and wearing them around the house to give yourself a relaxing footbath while you work is one that all fans of WLT's "The Tip-Top Club" seem to have remembered over the years, along with the idea that if you're depressed you should sit down and write a letter to yourself praising all of your good qualities, and the idea of puffing cigarette smoke at violets to prevent aphids.

Every evening, Sunday through Thursday, at 10:00 P.M. ("and now . . . direct from the Tip-Top studio in downtown Minneapolis . . ."), WLT played the Tip-Top theme song—

> Whenever you feel blue, think of something nice to do;
> That's the motto of the Tip-Top crew.
> Don't let it get you down, wear a smile and not a frown,
> And you'll be feeling tip-top too.

—and Bud Swenson came on the air with his friendly greeting: "Good evening, Tip-Toppers, and welcome to *your* show. This is your faithful recording secretary, chief cook and bottle-washer, Bud Swenson, calling the Club to order and waiting to hear from you." And of the hundreds of calls that came in on the Tip-Top line (847-8677, or T-I-P-T-O-P-S), and of the fifty or sixty that actually got on the air, many were from listeners who simply wanted Bud to know they were doing fine, feeling good, and enjoying the show. "And—oh, yes," they might add, "we got our boots on," referring to overshoes.

Every night, Bud got at least one request for a copy of the poem a woman had written about writing a letter to yourself. It was called "Dear Me," it was a hundred and eight lines long, WLT mailed out 18,000 copies of it in the six months after it was written (May 18, 1956), and it began:

> When I look around these days
> And hear blame instead of praise
> (For to bless is so much harder than to damn),
> It makes me feel much better
> To write myself a letter
> And tell myself how good I really am.
>
> Dear Me, Sorry it's been
> So long since I took pen
> In hand and scribbled off a word or two.
> I'm busy with my work and such,
> But I need to keep in touch
> Cause the very closest friend I have is you.
>
> Through times of strife and toil,
> You've always remained loyal
> And stuck with me when other friends were far,
> And because we are so close,
> I think of you the most
> And of just how near and dear to me you are.

As for puffing smoke at violets, it touched off a debate that lasted for years. For months after it was suggested by an elderly woman, Bud got call after call from listeners who said that smoke-puffing would *not* discourage aphids; that even if it would, there are *better* ways to discourage aphids; and, worse, that it might encourage young people to take up smoking.

The pro-puffers replied hotly that: (1) you don't have to *inhale* in order to *puff* on a plant; (2) the treatment should be given only once a week or so; and (3) anyone who wants to smoke probably will go ahead and do it *anyway,* violets or *no* violets.

As time passed, the issue became confused in the minds of some Tip-Toppers, who came to think that Bud himself was a smoker (he was not). To the very end (November 26, 1969), he got calls from listeners wanting to know if he didn't agree with them that smoking is a filthy habit. (He did.)

At Bud's retirement party, Roy Elmore, Jr., president of WLT, presented him with twenty-five potted violet plants, one for each year of service.

Controversy was the very thing that distinguished "The Tip-Top Club." It had none. Edgar Elmore, the founder of WLT, abhorred controversy, and the terms of his will bound his heir, Roy Jr., to abhor it also. Though Edgar never heard Bud's show, having died in 1940, eleven years before the Club was formed, he certainly would have enjoyed it very much, as Roy Jr. told Bud frequently. No conversation about religion or politics was permitted, nor were callers allowed to be pessimistic or moody on the air. If a person started in to be moody, he or she was told firmly and politely to hang up and *listen* to the show and it would cheer him or her up. Few had to be told.

Vacations and pets were favorite Tip-Top topics, along with household hints, children, gardening, memories of long ago, favorite foods, great persons, good health and how to keep it, and of course the weather. Even when the weather was bad, even in times of national crisis, the Tip-Toppers always came up with cheerful things to talk about.

One reason for the show's cheery quality and the almost complete absence of crank calls was Bud's phone policy. After the first year he never divulged the Tip-Top phone number over the air (nor, for that matter, over the phone). In fact, it was an unlisted number, and one could obtain it only from another Tip-Topper. This tended to limit participation to those who understood the rules and accepted them.

The main reason for the show's cheery quality was Bud himself and his radio personality. His voice wasn't deep but his style of speaking was warm and reassuring, and he always tried to look on the bright side, even as host of "The Ten o'Clock News" (starting July 1, 1944). On the newscast, Bud played up features and human-interest stories and he skimmed over what he called "the grim stuff." He might devote fifteen seconds to a major earthquake and three minutes to a story about a chimpanzee whose finger paintings had been exhibited at a New York gallery and fooled all the critics. His approach offended a few listeners ("the *New York Times* crowd," he called them), but most people liked it. Bud pulled in fifty or sixty fan letters a week, more than all other WLT newscasters combined.

After reading a few headlines, he'd say, "Oh, here's something you might be interested in," and he'd tell about a dog that had actually learned to sing and sing on key, or read a story about the world's largest known tomato, or about a three-year-old kid who was a whiz at chess; and then he'd talk about a dog that *he* knew, or a kid *he* knew, or a tomato *he* had seen, and then he'd say, "Well, I don't know. Let me know what *you* think."

At first, some letters said, "What happened to the news?" but they quickly dwindled. ("Anger doesn't last," Roy Jr. said. "Only love is lasting. Angry people spout off once and then get over it. The people who love you are loyal to the end.") Most of the letters were about a story Bud had read: the letter writer described a similar experience that *he* had had, or quoted a poem or a saying that the story had reminded *her* of—and Bud made sure to read every one of those letters on the air. One day in the winter of 1950, Roy Jr. said, "It's time to close down the News. You need a new shingle."

According to Bud, the Tip-Top Club was the idea of a woman in St. Paul. "We love your show," she wrote in January 1951, "and feel that truly it is our show too. When I listen, as I do every night, I feel as if I am among friends and we are all members of a club that gathers around our radios. We share ideas and experiences, we inspire each other with beautiful thoughts, and I only wish I could meet personally every one of the wonderful people who also write to you, for when they write to you, they are truly writing to me also."

Bud read her letter on the air, and listeners responded favorably to the idea of a club. (Since he had often referred to his stories as "News-Toppers," Bud suggested the name Tip-Top Club and it stuck.)

Nobody at WLT quite remembers who came up with the phone idea. WLT had been doing remote broadcasts over telephone lines for years, starting with the "WLT Barn Dance and Bean Feed" in 1938; all that needed to be done to put a telephone signal on the air was wrap the bare end of one wire around the bare end of another. One night, Bud's engineer, Harlan, did just that, and a woman's voice came on describing dark thunderstorm clouds moving east toward Minneapolis.

"Is it raining there yet?" asked Bud.

"No," she said, "but it will be, any minute now. But I've got my boots on!"

Roy Jr. was leery of the phone idea from the start. "Every

foulmouth in town will be slobbering into his telephone for the chance to get on the air," he told Bud. "Every creep who writes on toilet walls, every dummy, every drunken son-of-a-bitch from hell to breakfast. We'll be running a nuthouse. We'll lose our license in a week."

Then Harlan came forward with his tape loop. Harlan was one who seldom cracked a smile, but when WLT bought its first tape recorders, two big Ampexes, in 1949, he was like a boy with a new toy. He recorded everything on tape, and he played around with it, and his favorite game was to play around with Bud's voice. At first, he got a kick out of playing Bud's voice at a faster speed so he sounded like a hysterical woman; then backward, which sounded like Russian; then slower, so Bud sounded drunk; and then Harlan became fascinated with editing Bud. With a razor blade in hand, Harlan went through thousands of feet of Bud tape, finding a word here and a word there, and a vowel sound here and a consonant there, making new words, and snipping and splicing hundreds of little bits of tape to form a few sentences spoken in Bud's own voice, in which Bud spoke, in his own warm and reassuring tones, about having carnal relations with dogs, cats, tomatoes, small boys, chimpanzees, overshoes, fruit jars, lawn mowers. It was disgusting, and also an amazing feat of patience. In two years, Harlan assembled just three minutes of Bud.

Harlan solved the problem of loonies by the simple trick of threading a continuous loop of tape through two machines sitting side by side. Bud and his telephone caller could be recorded on the first machine, which fed the tape to the second machine, which played it back on the air three seconds later. If the caller said something not befitting the show, Harlan, listening to the first machine, would have three seconds in which to turn off the second. "Can't beat it," said Harlan. "I hit the button and they die like rats."

Nevertheless, Roy Jr. was on hand for the first taped show and supervised the Stop button personally. "I trust you," he told Harlan, "but the way you talk, you might not notice profanity until it is too late." Bud explained the tape loop on the air and invited calls as Roy Jr. hunched over the machine, his finger in position, like a ship's gunner waiting for incoming aircraft. The first caller was a man who wanted to know more about the loop and if it might have useful applications in the home. He got flustered in mid-call and stopped. On his radio at home, he heard his own voice, delayed by tape, saying what he had said three seconds before. "Please turn your radio down," Bud said. It was a line that he was to repeat thousands of times in the next eighteen years.

"This has been an historic event," Roy Jr. said proudly when the show was over. He had cut off just two calls, the first one after the words "What in hell—" and the second at the mention of the Pope ("Probably nothing, but I wasn't about to take chances," he explained to Harlan).

Most of the calls were about the tape loop, with all callers favoring its use, howbeit with some trepidation that a mechanical failure or employee carelessness might lead to tragedy. Several were worried that certain persons might try to fool Bud, opening their calls with a few innocuous remarks and then slipping in a fast one. ("Thanks for the tip," said Bud. "I'm confident we can handle them.")

Communists, people agreed, might be particularly adept at subverting the tape loop. Communists, one man reported, learned these techniques at special schools, including how to insinuate their beliefs into a conversation without anyone being the wiser. ("Appreciate your concern, sir, and, believe me, we'll be on guard.")

It was three weeks before Roy Jr. turned over the guard duty to Harlan and Alice the switchboard girl. Alice was to screen all callers: no kids, no foreign accents, and nobody who seemed unusually intense or determined to get on the air. Harlan was the second line of defense. Roy Jr. instructed him to listen carefully to each call and try to anticipate what the caller was driving at; and if the conversation should drift toward deep waters—hit the button. No politics. No religion except for general belief in the Almighty, thankfulness for His gifts, wonder at His creation, etc. No criticism of others, not even the caller's kith and kin. Roy Jr. didn't want them to get dragged into family squabbles and maybe have to give equal time to a miffed husband or mother-in-law giving *their* side of it. No promotion of products, services, clubs, fund drives, or events.

"What's left to talk about?" Harlan wondered. "Not a goddamn helluva lot."

And, at first, the Tip-Toppers seemed unsure of what to talk about too. "Just thought I'd call and say hi," one would say. "Great. What are you doing tonight?" Bud would ask. "Oh, not much," the caller would reply. "Just sitting here listening to the show."

Gradually, though, they loosened up, and when Bud said to a caller, "Tell me about yourself," the caller generally did. Most Tip-Toppers seemed to be older persons leading quiet lives and keeping busy with hobbies and children and grandchildren, and, judging from the interest in household hints, their homes were neat as a pin and in good repair. They were unfailingly courteous ("The distinguished gentleman who spoke earlier on cats was very well-informed on most points, but I feel he may have overlooked the fact that cats will not shed if brushed regularly"), and soon Harlan was taking his finger off the button and relaxing in the control room and even leaving for a smoke now and then. The few nuts who called in Alice soon recognized by voice— she enjoyed talking with them, and after a few conversations they always asked for her and not for Bud. They sent her gifts, usually pamphlets or books but occasionally a box of cookies or a cake, which, on Harlan's advice, she did not eat. Three months went by, and not a single nut got past the loop; Roy Jr. raised Bud's salary and even gave him a contract—six months with an option of renewing for three more.

"It is so pleasant in this day and age when we are subjected to so much dissension and mud-slinging to take a rest and listen to a show that follows the old adage 'If you can't say something nice, don't say anything at all,'" a woman wrote to Bud. "I am a faithful listener-in and now have a telephone in my bedroom so that I can participate after turning in. I go to sleep listening to the show, and I believe I sleep better knowing it is there."

Sleep was a major item on the Tip-Top agenda: how much is needed? how to get it? what position is best? Many scorned the eight-hour quota as wasteful and self-indulgent and said four or five is enough for any adult. "The secret of longevity is to stay out of bed," said one oldster.

Most members disagreed; they felt they needed more sleep, and one call asking for a cure for insomnia would set off an avalanche of sleep tips—warm milk, a hot bath, a brisk walk, a brief prayer, a mild barbiturate—each of which had gotten the caller through some difficult nights. A doctor (he called in often, usually to settle somebody's hash on the value of vitamins, chiropractic medicine, and vegetarian diets) offered the opinion that worry causes 95 percent of all sleeplessness. He suggested that Tip-Toppers who go to bed with restless thoughts should fill their minds instead with pleasant memories and plans for vacations.

As for vacations, there were strong voices in the Club who argued that a Minnesotan's vacation money should be kept at home, not spent abroad. The rest of the world, it was said, could be seen perfectly well in the pages of the *National Geographic*. There was general agreement, however, that the purpose of a vacation is to rest and enjoy yourself and not necessarily to visit family members or to catch up on work around the house.

Housework was important, though, a sure antidote for grief and worry and feeling sorry for yourself. To scrub a floor or paint a wall or make a pie was better than going to a psychiatrist. At the same time, there was no use taking more time than necessary to get the job done, and every job had its shortcuts. "What's a quick way to get bubble gum out of hair?" a woman would ask, and minutes later, a legion of women who had faced that very problem would rally to her side. Give the Club a problem, and in short order the Club solved it, whether it be a wobbly table, a grape-juice stain, or a treacherous stair tread, and then it suggested two or three things you could do in the time you had saved, such as making lovely and useful gifts from egg cartons, Popsicle sticks, and bottle caps.

And then there were hobbies. Bud often asked callers, particularly the shyer ones, to talk about their hobbies. He *never* asked about their occupations, not after the first few times: the answers were always apologetic-sounding—"Oh, I'm just a truck driver," or "Oh, I just work for the Post Office." But ask someone what he did in his spare time and the answer might be good for five or ten minutes.

Club members tended to be collectors. It seemed as if every object of which there was more than one sort, type, shape, brand, color, or configuration was the object of some collector's affection. "I have matchbook covers from more than thirty-five countries." "Some of my fruit jars have been appraised at ten dollars and more." "I hope someday to open a license-plate museum." "I plan to donate my nails to the historical society."

Bird-watching, a sort of collecting, was also popular, and Bud had to put a damper on the bird people, they were so fanatical. One might call in and say, "I wonder if anyone out there can help me identify a bird I heard this morning. Its call sounded something like this—" and then whistle, *"twee-twee, twee-twee,"* and suddenly Alice was swamped with calls, some identifying the bird, some saying they had heard it too and didn't know what it was either, and others wondering if the bird's call perhaps wasn't more of a *"twee-it, twee-it."*

Five nights a week, from 10:00 P.M. to sign-off, Bud sat in Studio B behind a table, the earphones clamped on, and scribbled notes on a pad as one Tip-Topper after another poured it out. After the first few months of the tape loop, he quit reading news stories, and after the Club had hit full stride, telephonically speaking, he himself said very little, aside from an occasional question. He became a listener. For eighteen years, from 1951 to 1969, he sat in the same chair, in the same position (slightly hunched, head down and supported with one hand, the other hand writing, feet on the floor), and heard the same stuff, until he seemed to lose whatever personality he had in the beginning. He became neutral. "A goddamn ghost," Harlan said. "When he comes in, I don't even see him anymore. He don't really exist, except on the air."

At the age of sixty-five, he quietly retired. He didn't mention his retirement on "The Tip-Top Club." Tip-Toppers didn't know he was gone until they tuned in one night and heard Wayne Bargy. Wayne was the only WLT announcer willing to take the show. Others had subbed for Bud before when he took vacations and they noted a certain snideness, a meanness, among the Tip-Toppers, who implied in their conversations that the new man, while adequate, was certainly no Bud. "Bud would *know* that," a caller might say. "Bud wouldn't have said that." "Maybe I'll talk to Bud about it. When is Bud coming back?"

So one night out of the clear blue it was "The Tip-Top Club with Wayne Bargy," and one can only imagine the shock that Bud's fans felt to hear a new theme song (Simon and Garfunkel's "Sounds of Silence") instead of the old Tip-Top song, and then

Wayne Bargy delivering a tribute to Bud as if Bud were dead. He called him "an innovator" and "a genius" and "a man who was totally concerned about others." "I loved him," said Wayne. "He was a totally understanding, giving type of man. He was someone I could always talk to about my problems.

"Friends, I know you're as disappointed as I am that Bud won't be here with us anymore, and let me tell you, I'd give anything if he were, and I want to be honest with you and admit that I've never done this type of show before and I don't know how good I am at talking with people, and maybe some of you will even wonder what I'm doing in the radio business and I have to admit that you may have a point there, but I would rather be honest about this than sit here and pretend that I'm somebody that I'm not, because I think that honesty has a place in radio, I don't think a radio personality has to be some sort of star or an idol or anything, I think he can be a real person, and even if I should fail and would quit this show tomorrow, I'd still be satisfied knowing I had done it my way and not tried to be like somebody else."

The Tip-Toppers heard him out; there was a minute or so of lull at the switchboard (perhaps they were too dazed to dial, or else they were composing carefully what they would say); and then the first wave struck. Even Harlan was surprised by the abuse Wayne got.

First call: "Why wait until tomorrow? Why not quit to-night?" (Wayne: "Thanks for calling.") A man said, "Oh, don't worry that we'll consider you a star, Wayne. Don't worry about that for one minute!" (Wayne: "Okay, I won't.") A woman said it was the worst night of her life. (Wayne: "It's hard for all of us.") "You make me absolutely sick. You're the biggest mistake they've made down there!" ("I appreciate your honesty, sir. I don't necessarily agree with that statement, but I think it's important that you feel you can be honest with me.")

By midnight, Wayne had logged almost a hundred calls,

most of them quite brief and most cut off by Harlan. The longest exchange was with a woman who wanted to know where Bud was. Wayne said that Bud had retired.

SHE: Then I'd like his number.
HE: I'm sorry?
SHE: I want Bud's phone number.
HE: I—ma'am, I wish I could give you that but I can't, it's against company policy. We don't give out announcers' home numbers to the general public.
SHE: Well, *I'm* not the general public. I'm Grace Ritter and he knows me even if you don't.
HE: I'm sorry, but—
SHE: And this is his show, and I think he has a right to know what you're doing to it! (CLICK)

During the midnight newscast, Roy Jr. called and told Wayne he was doing great. "I knew it'd be tough sledding the first night," he said, "but you stick in there. They're sore about Bud, but in three weeks they'll get tired and give up and all you'll get is flowers."

It didn't work that way. For one thing, Wayne had little interest in the old Tip-Top topics. He was divorced and lived in an efficiency apartment (no lawn to keep up, no maintenance responsibilities) and had no pets or children. His major interest was psychology. "People fascinate me," he said. ("You don't fascinate *me*," someone said.) He read psychology books and talked about them on the air. He said that he was undergoing therapy, and it had helped him to understand himself better. ("What's to understand?")

His other interests were eating out in foreign restaurants, attending films, and planning a trip to the Far East. ("How about leaving tomorrow?") Occasionally, he got a friendly caller who also liked Szechuan cuisine or Carl Rogers or Woody Allen movies, and he reached out and hung onto that call for dear life. Those calls would last for fifteen, twenty minutes, as if the caller were an old college chum he hadn't heard from in ages, but when he hung up, the Tip-Toppers were waiting, more determined than ever.

THEM: This show is so boring. You talk about stuff that nobody but you is interested in.

HIM: I really think you're mistaken about that, at least I hope you are, but more importantly, I think that I would have no business being here if I *didn't* talk about things that interest me, because, when all is said and done, I do have to be myself.

THEM: That's the problem, Wayne. Yourself. You're dull.

HIM: Well, I grant you I'm not slick or polished, and I'm not a comedian, but that's not my job. Basically, I'm a communicator, and whatever my faults or failures in relating to people, I do try to be positive.

THEM: You're positively boring.

HIM: Well, let's talk about that. Define your terms. What do you mean by "boring"?

What they meant was Wayne Bargy. For all he said about keeping an open mind ("You got a hole in your head, Wayne!") and not condemning others but trying to understand people who may be different from ourselves ("You're different from everybody, Wayne! You're a different species!"), the Club kept a united front against him.

One night, Wayne casually mentioned that it was his first anniversary hosting the show. The switchboard sizzled. One man said it was time for Club members to take action, and before Harlan could cut him off he announced a time and a place for the meeting.

Word came back that the Tip-Toppers had elected officers and were putting together a mailing list for a monthly newsletter. It was said the Club was assigning members to "listening squads" with each squad assigned two hours of "Wayne duty" a week. The squad members were responsible for listening to the show and calling in frequently. The newsletter printed a list of things to say.

It was harder on Harlan than on Wayne. Harlan had started to assemble a special Wayne Bargy tape, but he had no time to work on it. What with Wayne giving out the phone number every fifteen minutes, the show was attracting oddballs, in addition to the legions of Tip-Toppers, and Harlan was cutting calls off the air by the dozens. One night, after Wayne had talked about his divorce (he said that he and his wife didn't "relate to each other sexually"), there passed a long half hour during which no call was fit to broadcast. "I was slapping them down like barnyard flies. We were up to our ears in crazies," said Harlan. "Finally, my fingers got sore, and Alice pulled the plug on the switchboard and her and me sat down and had a cup of coffee and left that poor dumb SOB sit and die by himself."

Wayne talked a long time that night. He said he'd had a typical middle-class upbringing until he went to college, which opened his mind up to new possibilities. He said he had gone into radio because it had tremendous possibilities for creative communication. This show was a tremendous opportunity to get people to open up their minds. He viewed himself as an educator of sorts.

"I'll be honest," he said. "The past year has been rough. There's a lot of anger and violence out there—and I don't say people shouldn't feel that way, but I do feel people should be willing to change. Life is change. We all change. I've changed. Frankly, when I started doing this show, I didn't come off very well. I didn't communicate well. I had a hard time relating to working-class people. I think I've improved. I'm learning. I've put my feelings on the line, and I've benefited from it. I'm going to keep on trying."

He did keep on trying, and the Tip-Toppers kept calling— "We won't go away, Wayne!" they said, and he said, "I don't want you to go away. I want you to stay and let's get to know each other." That summer WLT did a survey that showed that most of the Tip-Top Club audience was over forty (72 percent), the least desirable age group to advertisers, and in July the station switched the Tip-Top slot to what it called "a modified middle-of-the-road pop-rock format" with a disc jockey who never talked except to give time, temperature, and commercials. His name was Michael Keske, but he never said it on the air.

JACK SCHMIDT ON THE
BURNING SANDS

A "Jack Schmidt, Arts Administrator"
Adventure

In the almost six years since I slipped the private-eye game to
become an ace artsman in Minneapolis, I have regretted the
career change approximately once, that being the A.A.A.A.
Conference in Puerto Vallarta last fall at which I was strong-
armed into speaking on "Priorities in Programming: The Commitment to Communication and the Question of Quality." It
was my first trip to Lecternland, and I remember it as clearly
as the time my secretary Bobby Jo put creosote in my panatela.

I am not your arts administrator who dotes on hearing his
voice amplified talking about things that begin with the same
letter. I am not big on conferences in general or anything else
that involves sitting in a hotel banquet room and looking at

chicken Kiev and creamed peas while some flyweight talks about
the importance of innovation.

For one thing, I saw enough of hotels in my previous line of
work (*The Tomato in 204, Murder from Room Service, The Magic
Fingers Gang, Dead Man: Do Not Disturb, Mr. Chatworth Checks
Out,* etc.); and for another, the sensitive souls who address these
galas tend to tiptoe around the main idea, which is Money.
Large sums of cash lie trapped in banks and want to see the
world—meanwhile, there are swell artistes who would love
someone to put a wad in their smocks without them noticing
it. And who wouldn't mind one bit if he kept some to cover
his highly innovative operating expenses. That is the A. and
the B. of arts administration, the "Let me begin by pointing
out" and the "Let me conclude by saying," and it's all done
back at my office in the Acme Building and not in the Chry-
santhemum Room of the Hotel Coffin. I sit down to listen to
speeches and all I hear is my phone going unanswered.

On this particular day, however, the phone was silent, a mere
objet d'interest in a deskscape as barren as all outdoors. It was a
Monday in January, the sort of bitterly cold day that the Minneapolis Chamber of Commerce tries to keep secret, when house-
plants keel over and dead cars line the streets and anyone with
sense is heading for the airport. I trudged the six blocks from
the Whispering Arms to the Acme Building, made coffee, and
drank three boiling cups before I was aware of physical sensation.
I wrung my hands to make sure they were there. I counted my
feet.

I had hit bottom, the depths, the Zasu Pitts, the Rudy Vallee,
the utter Ralph Nader of my existence.

It all began back in December with a visit from Roland
Smollett—Roland Smollett the massage-parlor magnate, a pa-
riah in polite society and a stranger to culture until I extracted

fifty grand from him and sat him on the Board of Directors of the Twin Cities ArtStrip. My Board of Directors and my ArtStrip. Six miles of abandoned interstate renovated by yours truly to make the country's first drive-through cultural center.

He perched on my couch and sent me a little smile all the way across the room. "I'm here as friend and also on behalf of the board," he whistled. "Our thinking is that you need some time to rest, to gain breadth, to reassess direction." He went on for a few seconds about my unique contributions, my restless genius, my unending commitment to quality growth; and when he was done rhapsodizing, the upshot was that I was fired. Sacked, cashiered, canned, cut loose and set adrift with a little severance pay and a $2,000 grant from a program to help arts administrators rethink their mid-life priorities. That was my thanks for building "the most creative arts project in the past three years," according to the American Automobile Association.

He slunk out and I headed for Bobby Jo's desk and sort of threw myself across it. We had been through a lot together and I knew that she, of all people, would understand the pain of being phased out. I groaned a great deep groan and pressed my lips against her neck. She swallowed and kept on typing.

"J.S.," she announced. "There's something I've been meaning to tell you for quite a long time now actually. I've been offered a job as Project Director of the Regional Novelists Touring Program. It pays well, and there's no typing involved; and I'm taking it."

(Ironically, I was the boy who put the novelists on their feet, by spending a long afternoon hustling funds from Mrs. R. Philip Posthlethwaite, widow of the Posthlethwaite Foundation founder, she being under the impression we were discussing botulism.)

I got to my feet and stood with my back to her for several

minutes, looking moistly out the window. It was a gray winter day, the sort of day when you half expect your heart to be broken. I searched long and hard for the right words; and when I finally turned around and said, "That's all right. Don't cry. I'm not crying. Go. Go quickly before you can say 'I'm sorry.' Like a wild thing that takes its freedom—go, fly—without looking back," she had gone. Three weeks had passed, with not so much as a "Hi," "Having wonderful time," or "Wish you were here."

I poured myself a fourth cup of java, sat in my parka and stared at the empty desk. I admired the fine craftsmanship that brought out the natural grain of the wood and also wondered how in hell was I going to make a living. I was depressed. Something had ended for me—call it "income"—and whatever it was that had started, it was getting worse fast. Word gets around in the arts colony when one of the drones is dying, and December had brought me nothing but rejection letters. (Acceptances come in little envelopes, rejections in humungous ones that hold your application, your supporting documents, and all the dust they can shake from their sandals.) Rejected: an Upper Midwest Regional Media Resources Center. Rejected: a proposal to endow a soprano for use in the schools. Rejected: a proposal to convert an apartment building into condominiums for lower- and middle-income poets. I decided it was time to take my liver to Luigi's for a good workout.

"You look lower than a mole's ankles," remarked Ollie, the elevator boy, as he took me down to the lobby. "Whatsamatter, Mr. Schmidt? You been seeing too many documentaries?" I explained how I had been bushwacked by Smollett, leaving out the Bobby Jo angle. "Gee," he commiserated. "I was going to show you this clipping, but now . . ." I snatched it from his hand.

It was a "Business Brief" from the *Minneapolis Intelligence*, and one look at it and my ears popped. "Take me up, Ollie," I snapped.

"SHEIKH SHOCKS SAX CENTER, SENDS $16M STOCK STIPEND" read the headline. Briefly, it stated that a member of the Omar Bhadi royal family had shipped some preferred to the National Center for the Saxophone in Teaneck, New Jersey. A graduate of Princeton, the sheikh apparently had whiled away his noncredit hours in smoke-filled roadhouses, and even now, half a world away, the cry of the saxophone held some special magic for him.

Back at my desk, I contemplated the clipping with an eye for detail born of an ear for distant jingling. The gift was anonymous (there being perhaps a passage in the Koran condemning men with pencil mustaches who play "Moonlight Serenade" on big horns), but I could imagine the giver, an old Nassoon exiled in his native land and forced to give up gin gimlets and close dancing, recalling with a generous heart his nights of long ago in the fun-filled twentieth century. Perhaps there were hundreds more where he came from: old Elis, Crimsons, Trojans, Gophers, now ensconced in excess splendor in tiny tribal kingdoms, tending the world's biggest cash flow, who would be only too happy to send a few shekels back to the Land of the Undergraduates.

I got up and walked calmly around my desk a few times, but the thought of oil money made my head spin like Tai Babilonia practicing camels. Talk about icebreakers! The years I had wasted squeezing dimes from foundations, and here I was, sitting on top of the greatest mother lode of arts funding since the invention of the tax write-off!

I leaned back in the old swivel chair, parked my size tens on the desk, lit a smoke, and exhaled, smiling. I am no dummy and the world is no bed of oysters but now and then a man breaks through the line, rolls a seven, and stands on the summit, and is entitled to sit back and take a warm, appreciative look at himself.

"You're a genius," I said matter-of-factly. "Oil. Now all you need is some type of idea. A proposal. A concept. A vehicle."

"Vehicle!" I jumped. "Did you say vehicle?"

Bingo! Television. Of course. Public television. The Petroleum Broadcasting System. Mobil, Exxon, Gulf, and all their high-powered British imports—Upstairs, Downstairs, indoors, outdoors, up hill and down dale, Henry the Eighth and Elizabeth the First and Alastair Cookie—well, maybe it's time for the sun to set on the ole BBC, thought I, time for Arabian nights—maybe a dramatic series on the Omar Bhadi royal family, like Henry except better—more wives, for one thing, plus terrific desert shots, exotic costumes, fabulous wealth, palace intrigues, etc. "If you liked *Lawrence of Arabia*, you'll love 'Abu the First.'" A thirteen-week series hosted by Omar Sharif. Technical advisers, the Nobles of the Mystic Shrine. Funding for this program provided by a grant from the Organization of Petroleum Exporting Countries.

I was scribbling all this down on the backs of envelopes as fast as a man can write whose hand is shaking, whose heart is tap dancing—I wrote down "$250,000," then crossed it out and wrote "$500,000" and eyeballed it for a moment and added "(estimated)." I figured OPEC wouldn't mind if their producer went a few thousand barrels over budget. Then I reached for the phone.

I called Apex Printing and ordered three reams of stationery. Jack Schmidt Productions. Same address. Cable: JASPRO. Then I called R. Mel Wyman in Laguna Beach, California.

I had met R. Mel the previous spring at a conference in Nassau on "The Language of Film: Why Can't Johnny See?" and between sessions we had gotten pretty thick over rum colas. Mel was there as the winner of six Sammies for his contribution to Saturday morning television as the head writer of "Chip and Dip," but he confessed to me that drama—adult drama—was his first love. "Jack," he whispered one night, drawing me aside into a dark corner, "I would give my left eyebrow for a chance to write for a mature audience." That was almost a year ago, but I still get twinges where he squeezed my shoulder.

When I reached him in Laguna Beach, he seemed a little hazy about our friendship, but he warmed up fast as I described the Bhadi series concept, and threw in some beautifuls and fantastics, and as soon as I mentioned "pilot" he jumped at the chance to write it.

In fact, he was so excited by the idea that he wanted to talk about money right away. (Evidently, he had forgotten all about his eyebrow offer.) "Jackie, I love you like a brother," he crooned. "There's nothing in this whole wide world I wouldn't do for you. That's why, instead of ten or twenty or fifty, I'm going to make it five for you, Snuggums." Five grand up front in a cashier's check on his desk before he put one sheet in his type-writer. I tried to interest him in a percentage of gross, but the mere thought of deferred payment made him moody. I was afraid he might hang up on me, and right then, he was my only hope in the script department. I mean, I know a lot of playwrights through my job and they are all of the experimental sort who would take the Bhadi idea for a starting point and wind up with a script that works in Jack Johnson, Amelia Earhart, Nijinsky, and John Wilkes Booth, and is set in a cathouse in Milwaukee.

So I said yes to the five and mailed it that same afternoon along with a note asking him to send me a rough draft as soon as possible. "Don't worry about polishing every line to a high gloss," I cautioned. "I am dealing with oil ministers, not English majors. Just flesh it in and we'll worry about nuance later."

My mouth was dry as I moistened the stamp, and the bitter

taste of mucilage seemed a portent of things to come. The five
cleaned me out—everything I had was in that envelope, staked
on a hunch, a phone call, a writer who had not mentioned the
word "deadline," and the generosity of a distant country where
my name rang no bells. I stood with my hand in the letter slot
for a couple minutes before I let go.

My personal résumé for January, February, and March would
have been on the spotty side had I applied for a job, which I
didn't, not that a job wouldn't have come in handy in respect
to minor details such as rent and groceries, though I did manage
to keep myself in smokes, free-lancing grant applications for
local arts outfits. Ever since I cracked the National Endowment
to the tune of a hundred thou for the Minneapolis Underwater
Ballet Company five years ago, I have been known in these parts
as a man who is handy with an idea; and when I hung out my
shingle as a writer in January, every orchestra, museum, and
theatre in town was after me, hoping I could provide that magic
sentence or phrase that rings up a row of cherries in Washington
or New York.

And I could. The trouble is, I'm an independent. To me,
selling ideas is like playing poker for a salary. For example—
middle of February, a public schools executive called me who
once had harsh words for my Past Tents touring arts history
program but who now was in deep trouble. "Schmidt," he
confided, "last fall we got thirty thousand dollars from HEW
to develop a black culture project. . . ." "So I heard," I inter-
jected. "Anyhow, it's now five months later, our steering committee is spinning its wheels, and I'm looking at the first of
May. If I don't have a project on paper by then, we have to
give back the money." He sounded like the president of the
Northfield bank, hearing horse hooves and seeing masked riders
pull up to the hitching rail.

I promised to do what I could, but five minutes later, when

lightning struck, I knew the idea was too good for him, and I was not about to go halves on it. By five o'clock, I had it typed up and the envelope shipped eastward dappled with Special Delivery stamps and with me for a return address. It was a nice piece of work.

"Blues in the Schools" I wrote after Name of Program, and after Description:

> A twelve-week experiential interdisciplinary folk arts residency program to furnish students in intermediate grades with authentic blues experiences through one-day, in-school lecture-demonstrations by recognized professional blues resource persons for the purpose of creating a deeper awareness of the richness and diversity of the American blues heritage.

To this I attached a two-page single-spaced supporting statement that I entitled "Meeting the Expressional Needs of the Pre-Adolescent." It was a beaut. Insofar as I understood it myself, it said that kids today are so expertly parented, they don't know why they are so miserable. The blues would show them why. This would make them happier. (Of course, I wrote it more scholarly, more *bel canto*, with more feints and passes and capework than I have space to include here. You'll just have to believe me. I may talk like a tough, but when it comes to money, I can write terrific.)

It was just clear enough to make a potential funder feel he was getting in on the ground floor of something possibly Major and give him the sweet smell of Being in the Forefront, but not so clear as to give him an excuse to quibble over details.

Three weeks later, my phone rang. It was a secretary in Washington. She asked me to hold, please, and I was kept on hold for the obligatory time, long enough to create a clear distinction between the holder and the holdee. Though I was perfectly clear on that already. The man who was waiting at the other end, holding a stopwatch, was a bum in my book but a bum who drops bread on the sidewalk, and I was only one of many arts-minded pigeons who dance around his ankles.

When he finally picked up the phone, he said he had read the Blues in the Schools proposal with a great deal of interest. He wished that he were in a position to fund it. He was strapped. He was over-extended. The cupboard was bare. His current bananas had already been allocated. He was helpless. He was sorry. Times were hard. There was no room at the inn. His hands were tied. The party was over. The train had left. The warrant was signed. There was no blood in the turnip. Time to pack it in, hang it up, knock off, call it quits, ring down the curtain, close up shop, give up hope, jump ship, turn tail, hit the road, and holler uncle.

Of course, I have taken part in this little mating dance many times, so I hung on, tossing in a few uh-huhs, and waited for the bridge.

Finally he paused. "I might," he ventured, speaking very softly so as not to break the mood—"I might be able to squeeze fifteen thousand out of Special Projects. It wouldn't be easy. I'd have to win over a couple of people here who, frankly, are not big fans of yours. I'd be putting my neck on the line. But maybe, as a favor.

"Of course," he added, "you would need to come up with matching funds."

Matching funds! The perpetual curse of the arts administrator! Fifteen thousand dangled before my eyes but before the load comes down my chute I have to scrounge up fifteen more. The girl says yes, but first I have to find a date for her ugly sister.

I knew for certain I had no funds of my own, neither matching nor clashing. It was the middle of March, and I'd been traveling steerage since before Christmas. The Acme Building had been curious for some time about my continued occupancy. Their collector, a throwback by the name of Waldo Nitti, had taken to visiting my office on a daily basis. Thanks to Ollie, who clanged the elevator door whenever the palooka was a passenger, I was able to switch off the lights, ram the deadbolt, and lie flat on the floor trying to keep my lymph nodes from throbbing too loudly.

"Schmidt!" he bellowed. "You're in there! I can smell you! You got a hot plate in there! Open up or I call the fire marshal!"

I did have a hot plate, though by March my meals required no heating. I was existing on breadsticks, potato chips, and candied-apple slices that Ollie smuggled out of the cafeteria downstairs, plus the Twinkie his mother packed every day in his lunch. In my file cabinet, held in reserve for an emergency, were four hundred plastic capsules of non-dairy whitener.

That month, Waldo turned off the heat and cut off the phone. He tried to stop the mail, and then I had a long talk with the mailman and learned that he had written a suitcaseful of poems and wanted to know if they were good or not. We worked out a deal: along with my mail, I received a dozen or so poems to criticize. So far as I could tell, they were just fine. I found something to like in every single one of them. When I contemplated losing my address, I liked them even more.

This address was in the files of every big giver in America; and though none of them was giving the mailman shoulder cramps at the moment, I knew what a change of address could mean. These guys don't send big checks to General Delivery, and they're leery of P.O. boxes and addresses that begin "In care of." Though, as I said, mail call was just a whisper for me. Half the letters were of the "You may already be a winner" variety, and the rest were dunning letters that long ago had changed from "Dear Customer, This past-due balance may have slipped your mind" to "Schmidt, we have the house surrounded."

The only letter I wanted was a big thick envelope from Laguna Beach; and as March segued into April, I began to worry that perhaps R. Mel had misunderstood my situation. Perhaps he had taken me for one of those high-flying TV producers who plant five-thousand-dollar advances like garden seeds and are happy if one now and then comes up pumpkins. Perhaps he assumed that I had farmed out the Omar Bhadi idea to eighteen or twenty writers at once, a race in which it would be good enough just to make an effort. I tormented myself with thoughts of R. Mel lounging in Laguna Beach churning out "Chip and Dip" scripts and thinking, "Oh yes, I really should get around to that pilot I promised, that . . . what *was* that? Something Arabian . . . Arabian horses? A shish-kebab western? Something for Roger Corman maybe. 'Bedouin Beach Blanket Dune Lust Ritual Muslim Murder Orgies'? 'Dark-Skinned Desert Beauties with the Hots'?" Then I imagined Mel saying, "What the hell, it's only the middle of April. No sweat. It's money in the bank."

I could wait no longer.

With $8.63 in loose change harvested from pay phones in which I had stuffed wads of paper up the coin returns, I called Laguna Beach and conferred with my writer.

"Spare me the apologies," I snarled. "Put whatever you have in the mail no matter how fragmentary, no matter how painful it is for you to part with it—no matter that it is just starting to jell, percolate, or come together—no matter that you need to live, sleep, breathe, and eat it for just a few more months. If I don't see something scriptlike in five days, I'm coming out there with some fragmentaries of my own. I'm a desperate man so be a sweetheart and get down to the post office." I gave out a bloodcurdling shriek that I learned from seeing Neville Brand eaten by ants, and hung up.

Four days later, the script arrived, accompanied by a note from Mel ("I'm heartbroken that you're taking this out of my hands just when . . . ," etc.). The script was more like an outline, actually. About six pages, triple-spaced, wide margins. The title was "The Sheikh and Mrs. Samson," and it concerned an O.B. prince who is sent to New London, Connecticut, for submarine training, his country having purchased a tender, and instantly falls in love with an American woman, who shucks her second hubby and learns to like lamb cooked very rare. "My darling," he murmurs, squeezing her hand in one Connecticut bivouac after another, as the camera zooms in on the flame of the candle. "This won't cause any problems for you at home, will it?" she inquires. "My being a divorcee and all?" He assures her their love is a cinch and a snap. "When my uncle the king gets to know you as a person and not as a two-time loser, he will see that I cannot be a submarine commander without the help of the woman I love."

At that point, the script trailed off into notes and scraps—"Search for great whale? (Whale oil)," Mel wrote. "Possible golden-fleece angle? King dies and prince returns to Bhadi for intrigue scenes, palace atmosphere, identity crisis? She follows (get Jane Alexander) him into desert—no playgirl but real trouper, sleeps on ground, eats bean curd (?), learns lingo. Weapons deal takes him to D.C., but she stays, becomes public health nurse, while he whoops it up in embassy. She loves him but loves people more. Last scene, she wires him—'Where's serum shipment?'—but he already spent money on high life. Reads cable, looks out window long time, then 50 people come for a cocktail party."

It was spotty, but I was in no shape to do a rewrite. I penciled in some notes in the margin—"May need touching up here" and "Let's talk about this"—and shipped it to Washington, to

the cultural affairs attaché at the Omar Bhadi embassy, and
touched Ollie for a C-note to get the phone out of hock, and
sat back and chewed my fingers.

I believe in the telephone. For me, the bad news comes in
envelopes and the good by wire; so having my phone back
certainly put the bloom in my cheeks even if I did have to
answer it in falsetto. "Mr. Schmidt is in conference," I warbled.
"Whom shall I say called?"

"Twink Tibbetts," he said, one fine May morning. "Of Tibbetts Properties, Inc. Jack knows me." Indeed I did. The richest
man on my Board of Directors and also the tightest. Twink had
a hard time writing zeroes. Three was his limit. I made a few
clicks with my tongue and said, "Twink! How the hell are
you?"

I soon sensed that he was not well at all. The ArtStrip was
in Dutch with the IRS, he confided, after Roland Smollett had
installed a nephew in my job who had spent a lot of dough in
dim light using a check-writing machine with a metal stamp
of Twink's signature. The nephew was missing on a trip to
work out some cultural exchanges with Colombia, and the feds
were offering Twink a spot in the laundry at Leavenworth. The
upshot was that he wanted me back, to start work the day before
yesterday, money no object. His pen was poised.

"I'll give it some thought," I remarked, "and let you know
in a few hours," and before the time was up the phone rang
and it was Bobby Jo. "God! It's good to hear your voice," she
cried before I could say anything. "I'm stuck in Rapid City.
Can you wire me bus fare?"

"What happened?" I asked understandingly.

"I been stood up. To make a long story short, the novelists
turned out to be a bunch of prose poets. Unpublished, natch.
They skipped town with the advance and left me here with a

liquor tab that read like *The Great Gatsby*. This is the only call I get to make so could you send the money right away so I can come back and never leave you again?"

I could feel her lips trembling against the mouthpiece. I got all choked up. "Breathe in the phone for me, darling," I whispered, and she did. It sounded like Niagara Falls. "It's been so long . . . so long . . . ," I observed. I put the phone to my heart so she could hear what she had done for me. in that department. It was almost more than she could bear. After giving me her current mailing address and several numbers where she could be reached, she hung up in a paroxysm of desire and anticipation.

Suddenly, life was coming back together for me, as it so often does in stories of this type; and I celebrated that night by taking Ollie to The Banquet of Pasha, a ritzy Middle Eastern restaurant where the patrons recline on cushions under a tent type of decor and allow Nubian beauties to bring them big slabs of U.S. prime sirloin and baked potatoes with sour cream.

"Geez, Mr. Schmidt, I guess maybe decadence isn't such a bad deal after all," Ollie sighed over dessert. "A fellow like myself who is putting himself through American Studies in night school—I'm startin' to think mebbe I have read too much Henry Thoreau, not enough Henry James. Heck, there's a whole *world* out there I'm a-startin' to git curious about. Mebbe I could be your Ishmael or somethin'."

The poor kid was three sheets to the wind. It was all I could do to shovel him into a cab. "Here's a ten-spot," I told the driver. "If he starts talking about Huckleberry Finn, ignore it. Take him home."

The day the call from Omar Bhadi came was a Tuesday in June, one of those steamy summer days when your clothes hang on you like wet towels and the phone feels like a bar of soap.

"Mr. Niles calling for Mr. Schmidt," said a woman's voice, and she put me on hold. I could tell he was no piker because it took him ten minutes to come to the phone; meantime the woman came on the line six times to announce his approach.

"This is Nick Niles," a deep voice blared at the other end. "Thanks for waiting, Mr.————," and he pronounced my name as if it were something he had found stuck to his shoe. "I'm calling about your script." Suddenly I remembered him. In *Mr. Chatworth Checks Out*, he and I kept each other under surveillance for two days from behind newspapers in the lobby of the Hotel Royalton. The man was a camel. I had a sinking feeling this would not be my afternoon.

"About this script. It was sent on to me by the Omar Bhadi embassy because I represent them here. I'm an expediter, so let's not beat around the bush. The script stinks. That's the long and the short of it. I say, forget it."

He sounded as if he had two other calls on hold, six people in the waiting room, and a car double-parked at the curb. I had to take my hat off to him. Nonetheless, I told him that I had a quarter-million to produce the series and was looking to Omar Bhadi to come up with the remaining half.

He drew a long breath. "I am authorized," he said, "to offer you five hundred dollars for expenses. But the script is a turkey. It is an affront to the government of Omar Bhadi. The payment would be in consideration of your forgetting about the whole thing and never writing another one."

"Five hundred to give up my right of free speech?" I recoiled. "A pittance to relinquish a precious birthright? Sir, you are not dealing with a mere artist. I am an arts administrator."

"Can the constitutional chitchat," he growled. "I got two gentlemen here in my office who take size forty-eight extra long and who don't know the First Amendment from Second Avenue. At the moment, I am writing your street address on a small slip of paper and drawing them a map. Two grand. My final offer."

"Well," I said thoughtfully. "What the heck, it's only an amendment. An afterthought. I'd feel a lot better, though, if that two grand was in the form of a retainer so I could show you what I can do. I could advise Omar Bhadi on cultural relations, arrange exchanges, maybe come up with some TV properties—" "The gentlemen are putting on their coats," he observed. "They are putting on their big black fedoras and reaching for the doorknob. Whoops! The doorknob came off in their hands. Luckily, it will take me only a minute to fix. Let me say this first. Five grand. Five grand on condition you forget the whole thing. That shouldn't be hard for a smart guy like you. What do you say? Do you want to give me an answer now, or would you rather wait a few weeks until you feel better?"

"I forgot the question," I mumbled. "What country did you say you represent?"

True to his word, Nick sent a man over that afternoon, a short man with a big suitcase full of small bills, and the next day I paid rent, paid Ollie, had my suit cleaned, and wired Bobby Jo air fare to San Francisco. Then I caught a plane myself. A week in a bayside spa, I figured, should bring out the best in both of us.

And it has. As I write this (on expensive guest stationery) from a balcony overlooking everything Tony Bennett traded his ticker for, I have a distinct impression that things are going Jack Schmidt's way. A few months of suffering and deprivation, and now Bobby Jo is tiptoeing in with a fresh bucket of ice and tonight we are going to hold a conference of our own and discuss innovation with a double bed for a dais.

The only fly in the soup (F.I.T.S.) is "Blues in the Schools." Word has reached me from Minneapolis that my blues resource person, Sleepy Bob Johnson, has drawn fire from a feminist coalition whose members have counted eighty-six references in his songs that are unsupportive of the dignity of women—and from a committee of church leaders who accuse Bob of proselytizing in the classroom on behalf of rambling, gambling, drinking, and messing around.

Another case for the ACLU. In the meantime, I am going to mosey down to the pool and practice floating.

MY NORTH DAKOTA
RAILROAD DAYS

O Engineer, I cannot hear her mighty whistle blow—
Have you seen the Prairie Queen, where did she go?

At present, our Brotherhood of North Dakota State Railroad
Employees is broke, flat busted, beat down, and a *sorrier* mess
than can be imagined even by a Railroad Man such as myself.
It would take a crew of trained Politicians two weeks working
split shifts to explain: (1) Why was our Pension Fund played
with and wiped out in 1948 in a burst of enthusiasm for sun-
flower futures (birdseed!) by a State Appointed Guardian who
had been drunk for twenty years? (2) Why was our Free Pass
Right stolen by Amtrak in broad daylight in June 1970 and
nobody told us until we were on board for the Annual Excursion
to Minot? (3) Why is our Brotherhood Office and Clubroom
here in Devils Lake, that the State solemnly promised to keep
up, cold in winter, along with that the toilet leaks, plaster is

cracked and falling daily in big chunks, the lock broken, the stove smokes, and all but three chairs bunged up and useless, so now we must move in with the Elks? And two or three other curious matters. But why should the Politicians bother? They know we had to be good and dumb to go on the Road in the first place and they are right. An old shack and a gold watch fob our total "Thank you" for years of service, plus an annuity hardly big enough to plug your nose, and yet we all stand up and sing like Children on a Picnic, and me as loud as the rest: "You may talk about your Santa Fee or the Wabash Cannonball, but the North Dakota Prairie Queen was the finest of them all!" Yes, she was Quite The Deal.

When I first heard the Call of the Road I guess was 1912 when I was twelve and the campaign train of President Theodore Roosevelt passed through my home town of Lakota, N.D., one warm September morning at 3:30 A.M. Lakota was strong for the Rough Rider and turned out *en force* at the Town Hall for a bean supper followed by musical presentations and speeches by everyone and his cousin. We had all night, it was only 8:30. There were contests of all sorts—foot-races and sheep judging and a sledge-pull of fifty yards between Lakota Grange and Volunteer Fire teams, each harnessed to a two-ton load—followed by a dance and the grand procession to the Depot and more speeches by all those left out in the first round. Finally it was almost time. The children were awakened, torches lit, and all of Lakota assembled on the platform. Far away, Roosevelt's train could be heard coming down the main line of the old Grand Forks & Minot.

It had been agreed we would shout in unison as the train passed and that this salute should be something quite brief and to the point but at the last minute it was decided that as a courtesy to the sleeping President we would delay the shout until the train had gone through. With a burst of steam and a shower of sparks and a mighty roar that shook the earth President Roosevelt's train came into town highballing west. I grabbed on to my Dad's leg and watched the swinging red lanterns on the last car disappear into the dark. Then up went the shout, "Welcome to Lakota! All Aboard with Roosevelt!" and they fired a shotgun and we went home to bed. Oh, I thought, if only I could be on that train it would be *something*. It was the Greatest Day in my life at that age and is still fresh in my memory.

Four years later I took over Mark Jonson's spot as newsboy on the Dakota Mail. Then worked for Mr. Jack Roy, the Lakota agent, and finally I became a Trainman in 1923 and Assistant Conductor in 1928. The Mail was a good old train and the Flyer too—the Best in the West—so when the GF&M became the North Dakota State Railroad (1930), of course they kept the old crews, and on March 10 I drew my Conductor's cap and braid from Mr. R. G. Houtek, President and General Manager, in person, and boarded the Prairie Queen in Fargo for her first run—the beginning of twelve great years for the most part, certainly for those of us who loved her.

She was new then and oh, what a Beauty. Blue the color of a clear summer sky, with dazzling white running stripes and a red-crown insignia of the N.D.S.R. or "Andy Yes Sir" as we called it, "Yes Sir" for short. Rosewood and spruce and mahogany trim, and crystal lamps, red and blue plush seats, brass fittings, the ceilings of molded copper with tiny electric stars, and underfoot a deep carpet of green and brown in all fourteen cars, each car named for a county—and me and Mr. Houtek giving the Highball as she steamed from Fargo station for Grand Forks, Minot, and Williston, full of Politicians, Railroad Bosses, and Canadian whiskey.

It was the Queen I loved and not the Yes Sir, so a full account of that bunch of crooks I will leave to someone with a strong stomach except to say that the North Dakota people had long been gouged and stripped by the Rail Monopolies to the point of agitation for state ownership, which was the battle cry of the Popular League when it made quite a dent in the 1928 election and scared the Railroads up a tree. One year and six months later, the spring of 1930, the Yes Sir was brought forth with great benedictions and anointing of feet, the Railroad Trust donating to the State the GF&M, plus the Queen, to be operated as the State Railroad by a Board of Directors to be appointed by the Governor and purchased by the Trust, which would make it the Greatest Train in the World, and operated all for the People's profit and welfare, minus a modest return on capital investment, etc., etc., and subject to other conditions, stipulations, understandings, etc. . . . Yes, that N.D.S.R. Charter was a wonder. Three volumes plus and not light reading even for the Lawyers, it was a by-God Tabernacle in the Desert, built just so and the parts joined tight, and great was the wealth thereof and all was pleasing in the eyes of the Law, including much that the human eye could not see: long strings and little traps and sieves and siphons built in by Houtek and his crack attorneys, besides which the Railroads' tax would be fixed low, and all to be in effect until three months before the Second Coming. But the State of North Dakota was helpless as an old maid asked to dance, and bought the deal on sight alone and overlooked the smell. It was hard times in a poor country, and the N.D.S.R. would give jobs to thousands, and the Queen would be a Great Draw and Natural Asset in a land with no mountains, forests, or ocean. Our people were then migrating in droves to the San Joaquin Valley, and this would help keep some home by showing that North Dakota could do great things.

I took this at one-half face value at first, my faith going down from there, but when you were on the Queen, boy, she took your mind away. She was the fastest thing on wheels—could hit 130 some places, and rode as smooth as if standing still. You see, North Dakota is a flat state, and then too Houtek spared no expense on tracks, so they were the best. We were proud of the fact she was the only train to ever carry a billiard table, and one could enjoy a good game anywhere on the route except one curve north of the Forks named the "Debs Transit" for its tendency to redistribute the balls. Many rode the Queen for the restfulness alone—in fact, we carried a special sleeper Friday nights out of Fargo and dropped it in Grand Forks for the eastbound to take back, arriving at Fargo at breakfast time. Many others were bound, summer and winter, for the Dakota Hot Springs resort and baths near Devils Lake, to take the health cure, but believe me, the real attraction was the Queen herself.

To the older person especially, who knew the privations of homesteading in the "little old sod shanty on the plains," a ride on the Queen was Heaven at Home, and we spared no effort to please the people. We were ever prepared to stop at pleasure's call, knowing the time could be made up quickly later. Not a day passed but what we would pull up four or five times so the people might stroll by the track to gather wild flowers or photograph scenic spots, the "Poplar Grove at the Geographical Center of North America," near Rugby, being a favorite. In season, we paused to hunt pheasant and duck, and west of the Forks slowed to a crawl, permitting passengers to troll in the adjacent Trans-Dakota Canal from the observation-car porch. Many towns along the line threw gala dinners and receptions for the Queen. A station agent would put out the message on a forked stick: "Knox invites you to dance Saturday," and we'd pick it up and go, of course, and bring one of our bands— the Kolachy Brothers, the Big Pisek Hot Band, Cecil Pootz and His Grafton Spuds, the Wonderbar Orchestra, and yes, the great Bill Baroon and His Paloreenies. We had the best playing

nightly in the dance car, The Club Dakota, and were happy to
share.

Yes, the trip was considered *quite* the deal then and fun for
one and all, and of course the fun didn't stop when the train
was in motion. In addition to billiards and poker, there were
regular meetings of the Camera, Norwegian, Kiwanis, Writers,
Old Settlers, and Fargo clubs. Liquor flowed at the bars, and
we had the Queen's own brand of spirits brewed in a "baggage
car" ahead. In the dining cars, one found culinary delights
beyond compare: Prairie Queen ribs with candied yams, sauer-
braten and hot potato salad, blueberry pancakes rolled in sugar,
sweet rhubarb pie, Polish peppers, and fresh canal fish. And
then there was Houtek, quite a fellow and a show in himself.

Houtek was a Railroad Baron and acted the part, but he liked
to make others feel important too, I will say that for him. He
kept his office back in the last Pullman, never missed a run,
and as the Board of Directors seldom caught him for a meeting,
ruled with a free hand. He walked through twice daily with
his black spaniel, General Sheridan, tasting the pie and rubbing
the nap and analyzing the liquor, and woe befall the man who
slipped from *his* standards, but to the faithful servant he extended an arm of Brotherhood and Trust. Seemed like his arm
was *always* around somebody, and always there was the smell
of his rich wool suit, the flash of a pinkie ring, a cloud of
Havana, and Houtek's barony voice saying you and him were
friends, understood each other, and knew what Railroading was
all about. No matter what your name, you were either Bill or
Jim to Houtek—I guess he liked those names—and you stayed
Bill or Jim and answered to it. I was a Jim.

Houtek had a grand manner. He wrote the souvenir booklet
that we gave free to passengers. "Men travel far and wide to
see and ride upon this Train," it said. "They marvel at its Speed,
its Comfort, its luxurious Appointments. Racing through the

Heartland of America, it strikes Confidence and Determination into the heart of every Native Son. Truly, it may be called

THE TRAIN OF THE CENTURY
AND
THE JEWEL OF THE PLAINS."

There were also two pages on the Hot Springs baths—how they cured arthritis and other ailments brought on by cold weather, and promoted restful nerves and invigorated the marital relationship—and a big spread on Houtek, pictured at the throttle: "North Dakota's Efficient Public Servant."

(Did we have any idea Houtek *owned* 36 percent interest in one of the biggest Hot Springs spas and held partnership in the Springs itself? No, but when this came out, about 1946, it was like we had always known it. In a way, it fitted him.)

Well, I will say this. Houtek was King, and when you rode his train, why, you felt like a Prince of the Realm, and all of us enjoyed it to the hilt and none would say a word against him on *that* account. When you rode the Prairie Queen, employee or paying customer, why, the state of North Dakota rolled along beneath your feet. You sipped Houtek's prize bourbon and looked out across at the farms dried up and the farmers still poking the dust—a little white house out in the middle of nowhere, and not a stick of shade, and a lady's pale face in the window, her raggedy kids lined up by the track where they'd put pennies, all of them wishing they could be on the great train—well, you did feel like a Prince with a noseful of diamonds or a Potentate on Tour, and I guess that's how we looked to them too. They probably thought we were *all* Houtek. As I say, I don't claim not to have enjoyed this as much as the next one. Or to understand it any better or think, Oh, it was Houtek, Houtek did it—we had no idea.

On account of her irregular schedule and high speed at night, the Prairie Queen killed more people in her twelve years than floods and blizzards put together. She must have wiped out half a county. Crossing-lights were rare items then and people just never got used to expecting her. A little bump was all we felt. We'd pull up slow in the night and back her up, me and a trainman walking alongside with flares, a mile or so back to the crossing. Most often, we'd find a little coupe, with a young couple in it, or an old farmer in a pickup, and most of the time they were busted up bad and beyond help. But now and then we'd find a breather and haul him up into a Pullman and go on to the next town, and it was amazing how he'd seem sort of awestruck, *proud* even, to have been hit by the Queen. Houtek would come to his bedside as we started up again, and lean down and shake the hand of the victim and shout, "You are aboard the Prairie Queen! You are going to be all right!" And the poor bleeding soul would look up with whatever sense he had left and sort of *thank* him. Oh, it was strange business and would tear at your heart to see it, but there it was. There it was.

And now this brings me to certain events of 1940 to '42.

One fine summer night in 1940, we attended an Indian Corn Dance near Minnewaukan. Houtek and I rounded up the stragglers near midnight and hiked back to the Queen through a horse pasture. We came up over a hill, climbed through some barbed wire, and there, far off, were the lights of the waiting Queen and the faint low hiss as the big ten-wheeler fired up. She lay out there in the dark looking like a whole city, and I felt like I just wanted to spend the rest of my life on our beautiful Prairie Queen.

Houtek saw this—he had been advising me on investments, telling me to put my extra dollars into chemicals because the war was coming and we would be in it soon—and he added, "By all means, don't invest in that," meaning the Queen.

"There is no chance of that, I'm afraid," I replied. "The Queen is owned by the State of North Dakota."

"Well, there is more to it than that," he said. "Just don't you get involved in it in any way. I have made a couple mistakes in that department—and they are going to cost me in the end."

That was about it, but even that little remark gave me a stir. Houtek was not one to gab about business. He always kept his hands in his pockets and had a pair of adder eyes for anyone whose mind should wander into the executive domain. For example, the Queen carried an extra "mail car" (which was not a mail car), which was kept locked and to which Houtek alone had a key. Now, every man on the Yes Sir roll knew that that car was full of Railroad files and papers. Many times we saw Houtek and his assistants take stuff out and put it in, but once, when a brave engineer asked him if indeed those were Railroad papers in there, Houtek gave him both eyes full-face and dead poison. "You keep your hand on the throttle, Jim, and I'll take care of the line," he said.

So we made it a habit not to see or hear too much. Oh, we thought the contracts were funny—some of us had to sign for loads of groceries and various other train supplies, and the prices were ridiculous—and we noticed all the Lawyers on board and the agents for companies nobody'd ever heard of. They were perfectly obvious. These were men who'd warm up their voices in the morning—those rolling Episcopalian tones—and then gather round and lie in wait for Houtek, spreading out their papers on a table in one of the dining cars and listening, heads down and tails up, waiting for his "Morning, gentlemen!" Then it was every man for himself.

They'd walk right up each other's backs to get close to Houtek's ear. They fussed over General Sheridan—what a fine dog he was, if he ever sired pups to let them know, and so forth and so on—and now and again Houtek would take one of these grifters and make a pet of *him*, let him eat at the Houtek table, give him some choice concession, or so we guessed.

And then, too, there was the thirty-five miles of track east of Williston that got heaved up in the 1941 thaw something awful and never did get fixed. The dining cars had to shut down on that stretch and the band took a break, for though the Queen slowed to yard speed, she rode as if in a cyclone. It was a nightmare, screeching and scraping and clattering along like an old milk train and everybody hanging on to the seats and it was shameful and just made you *sick* to see her suffer that way. And then there was a stretch east of Stanley, and later the whole Hillsboro section went bad. Now some thought the whole mess was due to the steel shortage—maybe some old rails hadn't been replaced. But in actual fact the rail was practically new, laid the previous summer and obviously not up to grade—inferior light-gauge rail you'd use for siding at a pillow factory, maybe. Why? We didn't ask why, nobody asked. We knew. Deep down in the marrow of his bones where it is dry and cold and he keeps a little hard common sense the size of buckshot, the Railroad Man knew. Houtek was a crook—how else could you figure it? A plain out-and-out thief and egg-sucker like every other Railroad Boss or Lawyer, though you still hear a few fellows speak fondly of "Old Hooty," and many North Dakotans today will solemnly swear the Queen would be running yet if Houtek had not been hog-tied by the Labor Unions! Yes, this was the line put out by the Republican newspapers—in an editorial paid for by the Trust and issued annually like a Valentine. Come spring and time for the Directors' meeting to set rates and see the books, those papers would say the Queen was losing money due to Political Interference. Time to give Free Enterprise room to do the Job, they'd say—the government knows nothing about running a Railroad, but here we have Politicians dictating from Bismarck decisions that are not sound Business Practice, such as featherbed work rules and lavish pension benefits for the B.N.D.S.R.E. freeloaders.

I am never surprised by anything I read in newspapers, nor do I blame them any more than I would hold a grudge against a goat. But just to set the record straight, the Yes Sir Board of Directors was strictly on the tit and regarded the Trust with humble piety and obedience and never sat but what it knelt, and as for the Brotherhood, why, it was about as powerful as the United Orphans & Widows. A Republican court had found us to be state employees and thus made it illegal for us to have collective bargaining or to strike. We were Houtek's Boy Scouts and that's gospel truth, but just you try telling truth to someone born and raised on a bed of lies. You can lay it at their feet, draw pictures, say it in Swedish, spread it with jelly, or put it in a knuckle sandwich—they will always think it was us in the Brotherhood that ran the Prairie Queen out of business.

Well, it wasn't. It was that bone-cracking rail east of Williston, to begin with, that busted the eggs in Houtek's basket. At the time, in the summer of 1942, I was absent—off fishing on the beautiful Lake Lakota with my good friend Ramon Kilgore— but as I understand it a loose coupling was spotted on a coach a few minutes before the Queen's scheduled departure from Williston. The yard crew took a long while deciding they couldn't fix it, and by the time the coach was pulled and the Queen remade, the Trainmaster hadn't time to make a final inspection. If he had, he surely would've seen the bolt was not dropped in the lock on the "mail car" door.

When the Queen hit bad track and went into her regular convulsions, the "mail car" bounced around, shaking loose the catch, and the door slid open. When she came to good track and the engineer put the coals to her—well, they say it was Houtek saw it first: what looked like a funnel cloud of paper boiling out of that car and up over the prairie, where a strong wind took hold and carried it off southeast. They say Houtek saw it and stood up and fell against the window and his knees buckled and he caught the emergency cord on the way down. They thought he was dead of a stroke. His face was blood-purple, and four men hauled him to his bed.

The Queen stopped there three hours on a little rise looking east, and every man, woman, and child aboard went out and combed the grass for loose paper. Oh, it was a sight, they say, how boxes jumped from the speeding train, fell to the ground, and burst like bombs, and the written history of the N.D.S.R., its coin, its harvest, its every bill of theft, the index of its lies, the worthless bonds, in short The Goods, all was released and flew away and scattered itself over thousands of square miles of North Dakota to be plowed under as compost, and so poisonous was the ink that crops were thin for years thereafter. Oh, I wish I had been there to see it, it was *something*!

Meanwhile, Houtek came to and went out of control. They had to lock him in his office with a bottle of whiskey and hope for the best. He was hollering and kicking the walls and firing people through the door, but then finally he calmed down and began to brood. Of course, it's only a guess, but I tend to think he got to missing all that paper something fierce now it was gone. Maybe he feared it was lost, maybe he feared it would be found, maybe he saw blackbirds swooping at his head and other voracious creatures come to meet him now that he had nothing to beat them back with, but mostly I think he just grieved. I believe he went some kind of loony in there, though among powerful men it is not so noticeable. He was silent, unlike himself, and wouldn't be roused.

"Mr. Houtek, shall we move?" the conductor called again

and again through the door. No answer. Up ahead, the engineer, "Captain Jim" Hinkley, hauled on the whistle, wanting to be off. Finally, orders or no, the Queen started up. Houtek stayed hid through Minot and was not seen until Devils Lake. It was dark and the yard lights were blacked out, but they say it was him who snuck from the Queen to the station office and stayed locked in there for twenty-five minutes, until a car came for him—a black Chrysler.

The scheduled stop was ten minutes and the Queen was set to leave when smoke was noticed coming from the "mail car." It was a smoldering fire. They had it almost put out, but it flamed up again, and all passengers were taken off as a precaution. Just then a Yes Sir detective appeared from the station— a short man with a big cigar—and took charge, said all crew was to report to the desk immediately, Houtek's orders. This was contrary to rules, to order the crew off a standing train, and Captain Jim demanded to have it in writing, so the detective wrote it on the back of a freight bill: "Crew relieved, Queen/ 11:24P by RGH." She was burning, the mail and the first baggage, and Jim was cursing and crying, but the old veteran took his orders and, with his fireman, Steve, stood off across the platform from his cab, and Houtek's man climbed in and he was shutting her down, loosing steam, they *thought*, and then she began to roll. They dashed for the engine, and Steve had one hand on the ladder when the dick stepped on his hand and jumped clear and fell on him, and 11:30 P.M. on June 14 the Prairie Queen slipped out of the station on her final journey.

The word went down the line that she was coming, and coming fast. In several towns, straw bales were piled on the tracks to slow her down, and in Lakota the Volunteer Fire Brigade stationed themselves with a pumper by the depot to cool off her firebox, but she came by going 60, her whistle moaning, and fire glowed in every window, and we knew, and some wept, that we would never see the Prairie Queen again.

The call went down to the Forks to open switches all the way to Fargo, but the great crowd that had gathered at the Debs Transit curve was not to be disappointed. They say she hit the curve at 80—some say 100—and her wheels screamed as she jumped the track. She dug a double furrow three feet deep in the ground, and flew from the high bank of the Red River. They say she was airborne for only four seconds but it seemed like a week. They say a million birds rose from the valley and all was suddenly silent but for the rush of wings and the cry of a child in the crowd, and then she hit water. Hit so hard, they say, she sent a three-foot wave two miles upstream and four down, and the steam was so thick the eastern shore could not be seen until noon of the next day. There, they say, rests the Prairie Queen today, and they say on a quiet day if you put your head underwater you can still hear the slow tolling of her bell rocked by the current and the groaning of her joints as she sinks ever deeper in the mud.

I have not done so myself, nor have I seen the wreck, though maybe I have looked in the wrong place. Nor did I see Houtek again, though I heard he died some years back in Minneapolis, where he had become rich again and a pillar of the community. Anyway, after a few years and the general excitement of the war, he was forgotten by the people of North Dakota—all except us. We sit in our shack, we old Railroad Boys, and now and then remember him to the extent of wishing him safely in Hell. May his soul be forever tormented by fire and his bones be dug up by dogs and dragged through the streets of Minneapolis, and God damn his name and wipe it from every account and take all his money and that of his heirs and put it in a Certified Check made out to the Brotherhood of North Dakota State Railroad Employees (B.N.D.S.R.E.).

2

ATTITUDE

Long ago I passed the point in life when major-league ballplayers begin to be younger than yourself. Now all of them are, except for a few aging trigenarians and a couple of quadros who don't get around on the fastball as well as they used to and who sit out the second games of doubleheaders. However, despite my age (thirty-nine), I am still active and have a lot of interests. One of them is slow-pitch softball, a game that lets me go through the motions of baseball without getting beaned or having to run too hard. I play on a pretty casual team, one that drinks beer on the bench and substitutes freely. If a player's wife or girlfriend wants to play, we give her a glove and send her out to right field, no questions asked, and if she lets a pop fly drop six feet in front of her, nobody agonizes over it.

Except me. This year. For the first time in my life, just as I am entering the dark twilight of my slow-pitch career, I find myself taking the game seriously. It isn't the bonehead play that bothers me especially—the pop fly that drops untouched, the slow roller juggled and the ball then heaved ten feet over the first baseman's head and into the next diamond, the routine singles that go through outfielders' legs for doubles and triples with gloves flung after them. No, it isn't our stone-glove fielding or pussyfoot base-running or limp-wristed hitting that gives me fits, though these have put us on the short end of some mighty ridiculous scores this summer. It's our attitude.

Bottom of the ninth, down 18–3, two outs, a man on first and a woman on third, and our third baseman strikes out. *Strikes out!* In slow-pitch, not even your grandmother strikes out, but this guy does, and after his third strike—a wild swing at a ball that bounces on the plate—he topples over in the dirt and lies flat on his back, laughing. *Laughing!*

Same game, earlier. They have the bases loaded. A weak grounder is hit toward our second baseperson. The runners are running. She picks up the ball, and she looks at them. She looks at first, at second, at home. We yell, "Throw it! Throw it!" and she throws it, underhand, at the pitcher, who has turned and run to back up the catcher. The ball rolls across the third-base line and under the bench. Three runs score. The batter, a fatso, chugs into second. The other team hoots and hollers, and what does she do? She shrugs and smiles ("Oh, silly me"); after all, it's only a game. Like the aforementioned strikeout artist, she treats her error as a joke. They have forgiven themselves instantly, which is unforgivable. It is *we* who should forgive them, who can say, "It's all right, it's only a game." They are supposed to throw up their hands and kick the dirt and hang their heads, as if this boner, even if it is their sixteenth of the afternoon—*this* is the one that really and truly breaks their hearts.

That attitude sweetens the game for everyone. The sinner

feels sweet remorse. The fatso feels some sense of accomplishment; this is no bunch of rumdums he forced into an error but a team with some class. We, the sinner's teammates, feel momentary anger at her—dumb! dumb play!—but then, seeing her grief, we sympathize with her in our hearts (any one of us might have made that mistake or one worse), and we yell encouragement, including the shortstop, who, moments before, dropped an easy throw for a force at second. "That's all right! Come on! We got 'em!" we yell. "Shake it off! These turkeys can't hit!" This makes us all feel good, even though the turkeys now lead us by ten runs. We're getting clobbered, but we have a winning attitude.

Let me say this about attitude: Each player is responsible for his or her own attitude, and to a considerable degree you can *create* a good attitude by doing certain little things on the field. These are certain little things that ballplayers do in the Bigs, and we ought to be doing them in the Slows.

1. When going up to bat, don't step right into the batter's box as if it were an elevator. The box is your turf, your stage. Take possession of it slowly and deliberately, starting with a lot of back-bending, knee-stretching, and torso-revolving in the on-deck circle. Then, approaching the box, stop outside it and tap the dirt off your spikes with your bat. You don't have spikes, you have sneakers, of course, but the significance of the tapping is the same. Then, upon entering the box, spit on the ground. It's a way of saying, "This here is mine. This is where I get my hits."

2. Spit frequently. Spit at all crucial moments. Spit correctly. Spit should be *blown*, not ptuied weakly with the lips, which often results in dribble. Spitting should convey forcefulness of purpose, concentration, pride. Spit down, not in the direction of others. Spit in the glove and on the fingers, especially after

making a real knucklehead play; it's a way of saying, "I dropped the ball because my glove was dry."

3. At bat and in the field, pick up dirt. Rub dirt in the fingers (especially after spitting on them). Toss dirt, as if testing the wind for velocity and direction. Smooth the dirt. Be involved with dirt. If no dirt is available (e.g., in the outfield), pluck tufts of grass. Fielders should be grooming their areas constantly between plays, flicking away tiny sticks and bits of gravel.

4. Take your time. Tie your laces. Confer with your teammates about possible situations that may arise and conceivable options in dealing with them. Extend the game. Three errors on three consecutive plays can be humiliating if the plays occur within the space of a couple of minutes, but if each error is separated from the next by extensive conferences on the mound, lace-tying, glove adjustments, and arguing close calls (if any), the effect on morale is minimized.

5. Talk. Not just an occasional "Let's get a hit now" but continuous rhythmic chatter, a flow of syllables: "Hey babe hey babe c'mon babe good stick now hey babe long tater take him downtown babe . . . hey good eye good eye."

Infield chatter is harder to maintain. Since the slow-pitch pitch is required to be a soft underhand lob, infielders hesitate to say, "Smoke him babe hey low heat hey throw it on the black babe chuck it in there back him up babe no hit no hit." Say it anyway.

6. One final rule, perhaps the most important of all: When your team is up and has made the third out, the batter and the players who were left on base do not come back to the bench for their gloves. *They remain on the field, and their teammates bring their gloves out to them.* This requires some organization and discipline, but it pays off big in morale. It says, "Although we're getting our pants knocked off, still we must conserve our energy."

Imagine that you have bobbled two fly balls in this rout and now you have just tried to stretch a single into a double and have been easily thrown out sliding into second base, where the base runner ahead of you had stopped. It was the third out and a dumb play, and your opponents smirk at you as they run off the field. You are the goat, a lonely and tragic figure sitting in the dirt. You curse yourself, jerking your head sharply forward. You stand up and kick the base. How miserable! How degrading! Your utter shame, though brief, bears silent testimony to the worthiness of your teammates, whom you have let down, and they appreciate it. They call out to you now as they take the field, and as the second baseman runs to his position he says, "Let's get 'em now," and tosses you your glove. Lowering your head, you trot slowly out to right. There you do some deep knee bends. You pick grass. You find a pebble and fling it into foul territory. As the first batter comes to the plate, you check the sun. You get set in your stance, poised to fly. Feet spread, hands on hips, you bend slightly at the waist and spit the expert spit of a veteran ballplayer—a player who has known the agony of defeat but who always bounces back, a player who has lost a stride on the base paths but can still make the big play.

This is *ball*, ladies and gentlemen. This is what it's all about.

AROUND THE HORNE
by Bill Horne

Note: Bill Horne is sick. Today's column is by Ed Farr.

It's always a temptation to second-guess a team and say where it went wrong, but it's been my philosophy not to kick a man when he's down and that goes for the Flyers, not that it wouldn't be easy to fault this player or that after losing so many games this year. I know it's considered smart in some circles to criticize the Dutchman for letting the younger ballplayers "get away with murder" who some say didn't have much so-called desire, but the season is over and I say, "Next year means new opportunities for personal growth. Let's rebuild in a spirit of optimism." In the meantime, perhaps I could make some constructive comments about the past season as one who knows the team well, having worked with the fellows on a one-to-one and group basis as manager since Dutch moved up to general manager after the Fourth of July doubleheader against Pierce.

First, a word to the fans. As Dutch pointed out last spring, the Flyers only needed confidence in themselves to succeed. I felt that they might've done so had the Flyer fans shown some patience, adopted a quietly supportive role, and not demanded instant victories. Instead, after a few defeats they became bitter. They booed every mistake, however unwitting, in effect sending the players the message "You are not O.K. You are bums." By the time I arrived, the players were uncertain whether they could play ball at all. Since then, we have made some progress in talking out these problems. Perhaps if the fans got to know us a little better, they could join us next year in a helpful partnership for dynamic change. That is the purpose of this article.

Pitching: It was obvious to everyone that the pitching was not as hard as it should've been this year. Fans were quick to blame laziness or overweight. But after working with the pitchers in intensive group sessions we found that all suffered to some extent from what we have come to call "pitcher's block." Convinced that the ball would be hit anyway, they unconsciously "took something off it" (the pitch) in delivery. Typical was one right-hander whom I'll call "Phil":

PHIL:
  They have always hit my knuckleball. At first I thought I was bringing my right leg over too far and dropping the elbow. But now I realize I'm withdrawing from the pitch—actually bringing both hands up in front of my face to avoid seeing it—and I don't get a good follow-through that way. I guess secretly I've always felt the knuckler was an old man's pitch and hesitated throwing it. The hesitation threw my timing way off. I guess the answer

is to accept that I *am* thirty-nine and can't reach back for the old fastball anymore. If I do, I tend to fall off the mound.

After talking with the pitchers, we agreed that pitching less hard was their way of punishing themselves for past losses and perpetuating their self-image as "bad" pitchers. We agreed that this was childish behavior, and we tried to write a new scenario, or game plan, in which the umpire was cast in the role of persecutor and a hard pitch in the strike zone would "hurt" him.

Unfortunately, we did not include the catcher (whom I'll call "Milt") in these sessions. Milt felt that the hard pitches were aimed at him personally and unconsciously tried to "escape" from them, which resulted in many passed balls. Later, after I benched him and we had more opportunity to talk, I learned that Milt's father had forced him into a catching role when he was quite young; that Milt caught his father's pitching in the driveway for practice, and whenever the boy made a mistake his father indicated disapproval by throwing harder; that Milt interpreted this as an attack on his masculinity, which he came to feel was passive and precarious and had to be defended from a crouch and, in the case of very hard pitches, by dodging to the side. With more counseling and perhaps more protective equipment, I feel that Milt can make a real contribution next year.

Hitting: Once again, the problem was obvious to everyone: Flyer hitting was consistently nonexistent. But rather than look for the cause of the zeroes, fans merely complained that the batters didn't "stand up to the pitcher" and took too many called strikes. We wanted to get the players' view of the situation, and so we asked each one to draw a picture of the way things looked to him when he came up to bat.

The pictures were very interesting. One drawing, which was typical of the rest, showed the batter hiding in a deep hole and the opposing pitcher towering over him from the top of a nearby hill (the mound). The entire field was uphill from the batter and the bases in the far distance were hundreds of yards apart.

This drawing was entitled "Safe at Home," which was just the clue we needed. Apparently, the batters did feel safer at home plate (perhaps by the very implication of its name), even if they were somewhat uncomfortable. One player ("Fred") expressed his feelings in a poem:

> The baseball flies straight
> At me. Heavy shoes are stuck.
> How can I get out?

Obviously, this player does not mind being "in the hole." He would rather be there and then be "called out" than take his chances on the base paths, where he could be "thrown out," "picked off," caught in a "squeeze," or even "stranded."

Unfortunately, I tried to meet these fears head on rather than work around them. I told the players they must "guard" home plate, which would be "wounded" by strike balls, by striking back at the pitches, and that they could prevent the bat from swinging and missing by "choking" it. This approach failed. If a hitter got one strike against him, he felt that home plate *had* been hurt and couldn't be hurt much more by two additional strikes. And the idea of rewarding base hits with positive strokes by the first-base coach—it just didn't work because the players who most needed this reinforcement never got to first base.

Next year, if the fans will help us create a less stressful environment at the ball park, I believe it will help give the hitters a better perspective of the field and their relation to it.

Fielding: The rural setting of Hay Stadium has been, on the whole, relaxing and beneficial, but its use during the week as a feedlot and pasture has resulted in an uneven playing surface, especially demoralizing for the infielders. However, not all errors were due to bad hops. Infielders spoke of the ball having "eyes" and seeking holes through which to bounce for base hits. And, while they believed they could not reach the ball, they were also fearful of it hitting them, an apparent contradiction.

It seemed pointless to berate players for mistakes that stemmed from deep-seated attitudes, to tell them to respond to grounders logically and not emotionally, and so we instituted a program of simple infield exercises stressing body awareness. Working without a batter or ball and simply concentrating on movement, the infielders practiced graceful fielding and throwing motions, making impossible catches and throwing accurately while off balance. Some have come along faster than others, but at least toward the end of the season there was more action in the infield, more fluidity, more lateralness, and fewer instances of players standing in position and throwing a glove at the ball as it bounded by.

Ironically, as other players improved, the outfielders seemed to become distant and moody and to feel resentful toward balls hit to them. Previously, the low standard of play in the infield had given them a pleasurable feeling of superiority: "The infielders might miss grounders, but *we* don't, even if we do drop a few flies!" Now, with crisper infield play and better pitching, the outfielders were left with less to occupy their time. They tended to withdraw from the game and to feel that we were expecting too much of them.

JIMMY:
I love baseball and I love being in the outfield. It's very relaxing. But then—bang!—there's a fly ball and everyone's yell-

ing, "It's yours, it's yours!" and suddenly I'm expected to perform wonders.

Catching a high fly looks a lot easier than it really is, especially when you realize that if you do catch it, it's nothing, an "easy out," but if you drop it you're a bum. People sitting in the bleachers looking at you and yelling and throwing stuff over the fence—I'm sick of it! I'm sick of being treated like an animal in the zoo!

Perhaps, I thought, we do tend to brutalize outfielders. We speak of a good one as being "fast as a gazelle" or having "the eyes of a hawk" or "an arm like a rifle," and talk in terms of outfielding *instinct*, rather than outfielding intelligence and wit and creativity. Perhaps it is time we became more aware that each player, whatever his strengths or weaknesses on the field, has many fine attributes as a person. Perhaps we should begin by recognizing those attributes and reinforcing self-esteem rather than concentrating entirely on a player's faults.

Take "Bill," for instance. For weeks, we hassled him for his mistakes at third base, trying to force him into the mold of a Brooks Robinson or a Harmon Killebrew and giving him no credit for his friendly, outgoing attitude and his concern for others and willingness to offer helpful advice to other players even as his own game suffered. In effect, we were telling him, "You're not O.K. You're just a player and not even a very good one. You bobble easy ones and you swing like an old lady. You bat ninth today, buddy." Last week, I came to a decision. I told Bill, "You are O.K. You're my manager for next year, and you'll make a darn good one. You've got good ideas and you're a darn good communicator. Good luck." So Bill will handle the day-to-day decisions, and I'll be general manager and devote more time to the overall outlook of the team. Dutch has been a good general manager and we owe a lot to him, and I feel he'll make an excellent president.

THE NEW BASEBALL

If it were merely a sport, baseball would enjoy the permanence and stability of ballet or checkers, but businessmen know that baseball must keep up with the times. Such innovations as artificial turf and the Astrodome were thought up by treasurers and have almost brought the game up to date. (To be precise, they have brought it up to June 11, 1971, according to the latest figures.) The next decade will see even more radical changes, and one can only wonder whether baseball's farseeing executives are aware of what lies just ahead.

Baseball flourished at a time when most people accepted the doctrine of predestination. Later, during the Depression and in the Second World War, baseball offered certitude to a confused nation. Since then, however, the writings of Sartre and Camus have made untenable our comfortable assumptions about "safe" and "out"; the excitement of observing players at a distance has diminished with the development of wide-screen movies; and a new time-space consciousness, ushered in by the Apollo moon shots, has rendered "power hitters" pathetically obsolete. Alas, a home run no longer rates as a "blast" even if it is "hit a mile."

In a simpler era, Ty Cobb came up to the plate in a mood of fierce determination, but today's players, aware of the diminishing importance of hitting the ball, are more content to *experience* at-batness. In the dugout, the athletes no longer discuss batting averages, girls, and the stock market but the swiftly changing dynamics and dialectics of the one-time "national pastime." In contemporary baseball, they agree, cause-and-effect sequentiality is giving way to simple concurrence of phenomena as the crisis in baseball's system of linear reaction brings on a new "system" of concentric and reflexive response, and the old stately inwardness of the game is losing out to, or giving in to, outwardness, or rather *away*ness; the static balance of baseball—pitcher vs. batter, base runner vs. infielder—will shortly slither into flow, and the crowd, not content to cheer the artifice of great hitters and pitchers, will rise in tribute to the natural organic unity of a scoreless game.

In a few years, the ultra-lively ball will be introduced, ending the game as we know it. Baseball fans will quickly tire of seeing thirty home runs in one game and will demand a complete restructuring. The first barrier to fall will be the outfield fence. The outfield will be extended up to ten or twelve miles, depending on local zoning. Baseball, which has always concentrated on the pitcher, will look outward to the horizon, and a period of exploration will occur as players wander over the hill to search for the ball. The "home-base" concept will be scrapped next, of course, along with the ball-and-strike construct, and the infield will become a mere appendix—a staging area or on-deck circle, as it were. Infielders will wait there for their turn, which, as often as not, will never come. Outfielders, on the other hand, will be free as antelope, roaming the farther regions for fly balls or, as the case may be, not for fly balls, the ball itself having changed. Its flight will be erratic and mysterious; a player will no longer be said to be "on the ball" or even "under the ball" but rather "near the ball"—in sight of it, perhaps circling it or viewing it curiously. The time scheme of baseball— three outs to a side, two sides to an inning, nine innings to a game—will be simplified by eliminating outs, sides, and innings, thus leaving the idea of the game itself whole and round, and people will play until the sun goes down or the cows come home.

In time, of course, the entire stadium setup will become useless as spectators are drawn into the playing area, and free participation will evolve as tasks become less specialized. This will lead to the disappearance of ballplayers as a performing elite. Players and spectators alike will wonder "What is happening?" and "Will it happen?" and "What do I do in either eventuality?" The umpires, who will have disappeared along with home plate, will return to baseball as friendly advisers, suggesting alternative courses of action, turns of phrase, avenues of thought. People will enjoy great freedom of opportunity, and some real-estate speculation will take place in deep center, most likely multiple-family housing and light commercial development.

HOW ARE THE LEGS, SAM?

Watch the pitch. Say to yourself, "This baby's mine." At the crack of the bat, get yourself moving. This is called "getting the good jump." If it looks like yours, try to get there ahead of it. Spread your arms to give yourself balance, and position yourself so the ball will hit you on the chest if you miss it. Automatically, your hands will make the catch. Above all, get the good jump.

	G	AB	H	E	BA
1965	1	4	2	1	.500
1966	1	5	2	1	.400
1967	Inactive				
1968	Inactive				
1969	Inactive				
1970	Inactive				

Lifetime totals: Not available

Let's talk about legs. It isn't human nature to play ball. The natural man doesn't stand under or in front of fast-moving, hard objects. Therefore, his legs must not only be strong enough to get him there, the legs must *want to* go. This is my big problem.

I tend to back away from fly balls. Even when I played work-up as a kid, I always backed off and took flies on the bounce. I hated to look bad dropping a high one. It was my dad who made me face up to the game. He took me over to Strub's parking lot and hit high ones until the street lights came on. He used two balls, so I couldn't loaf on the return throw.

My dad also taught me to throw from the shoulder—a smooth, unexaggerated motion, with a snap of the wrist to put the heat on the ball. I say you can tell something about a man's character from his throwing motion, and I appreciate all my dad did to make an honest man of me. I throw well today, years later, but I'm still shy around a pop fly and wish it were hit to somebody else. I lose my nerve at the last minute ("You've got it!"), and this is my big fault. I'm working on it.

I dropped one in 1965. A family picnic game. I'm playing first (I asked to), their last ups, with our side ahead by 2–1, and my cousin Eddy comes up and takes a wild cut at a soft outside spinner and lofts a pop-up eighty feet high—a short run to my left, foul. I moved over to catch it, but only medium quickly—understand? I pulled back from it and it fell off the tip of my glove. "It's O.K. We'll get this clown!" my dad yelled. He knew how much I hated myself right then. *I could have had it.*

One day the next summer, I was riding my bike around the lake when I heard a man shouting at me. An Indian fellow about forty wearing a purple softball uniform came chugging up alongside. "You play ball?" he said. "We need one more guy." I said I didn't have a glove. "We got extras," he said.

It's in the rule book of everyday, I guess, that you're allowed

to say no only once in a situation like that, so I followed him
back over the hill to the softball field. I pulled on a purple shirt
and trotted out to center, where the Indian wanted me. The
whole team was Indians, from the South Side A. C. The other
team was from the Sheet Metal Workers. I didn't know them.
No warm-up, so I'm standing there stiff as a post when the first
man up smacks a line drive that parked in my mitt without me
moving a step. I whipped it back to the second baseman, who
gave me a big cheer. In one minute, I'm in the game and already
have some credit with the Indians, who look to be bent on
playing 1.000 for the season. Nothing more that inning or the
next, but I'm feeling easy out there. Our diamond was one of
four that faced in toward the central point where I was standing,
and I could've played center field in four games at once and
liked it.

At this central point there was an iron storm-sewer grate. It
was no more than a low hump in the grass, but I began to
think about tripping over it, so in the third inning I backed
up and stood on top of it—understand? The old "shy" trick.
So I was playing too deep for a low line drive in the fourth that
drove in two runs. I ran right by it and had to turn around and
chase it down. I heaved the ball back to second so hard my
fingertips stung. I wanted to bite off my hand. I'd been thinking
I wanted to play ball, but I'd been fooling myself. A fellow can
fake everybody into thinking he's hustling when he's not even
in the game. Here I was, getting fat off the fat of the fattest
land in the world, and I wouldn't even put out for these Indians
who took me on their team. Eight other guys straining every
nerve, and the ball is hit to me, the sewer lounger.

I'm glad to say I got another chance. Seventh inning, we got
the game salted away 12–3, and here comes a pop fly that
doesn't hang like it should but drops like a bomb into the space
between me and the kid in right field, where I snagged it three

(two) feet off the ground, getting the good jump and going for it as if I'm either going to bury myself nose first in the prairie or else make the amazing grab I did make, and off-balance get off a hard submarine peg that almost caught the runner leaning off third.

That was my last ball game—maybe the last of my life. For four years, I've thought of myself as a ballplayer on the strength of that one game I stumbled into and trotted away from, feeling very good about myself. I've tried to get back. Wherever I go, I talk up a game and sometimes recruit almost enough people to play. A couple times they didn't show, and other times I dropped out knowing that the other guys were fun players and didn't want to get grass stains on their knees, stretching for the big play. Forget it.

I'd like to think I could make that 1966 catch again, but I know I couldn't. More and more this winter, my thoughts are with that old ballplayer—you know his name. Fifteen years in the majors and a great competitor, almost never a game he didn't make a play that made you feel faint. But this winter his friends are saying, "You're looking great, Sam." They didn't used to say this. He's worried about himself, thinking ahead to spring training, thinking, I got to start slow, build, can't rush it. But they don't pay you for not rushing it.

He remembers last spring—how after four weeks in uniform his body still wasn't interested in running. Going for the long ball, he had to send himself on ahead and then sort of throw back a line and pull his old body to the spot. Late in the spring, he came loose in the knees; he had an operation in June and was out for the season.

In the papers, the manager said how much they'd miss old Sam and how he'd be back for sure next year, but over a drink he offered him a job as a scout. He's thinking it over. As a scout, he'd still get to ride in first class, with lots of leg room and a stewardess right there; if you needed a drink, she could get to you quick. But nobody looks at scouts. The only reason people have looked at him—*studied* him—for all these years is because he played good ball. He liked it, and every time he turned on the steam back came the news he was good, as strong and quick as he ever was or would be.

I need to get back in shape. Without a serious game to push myself for, my body is getting numb at the ends. I work all day at a desk in a low room. When I get home and put my legs up on the hassock, I look at them and think, Well, there are my legs, I wonder how they're getting along nowadays. I mean to run some this winter, and with a little work I know the legs will come around and I will be in fine shape in the spring.

3

THE NEW WASHINGTON:
AN INSIDE STORY

Mr. Wick said he thought that economically pinched Americans of today enjoyed viewing the luxurious Washington way of life of the Reagan Administration members, much as Americans who suffered in the Depression enjoyed watching Hollywood stars in the movies. "During the Depression," said Mr. Wick, "when people were selling apples and factories were still and guys were jumping out windows because they lost everything, people would go to the movies. They loved those glamour pictures showing people driving beautiful cars and women in beautiful gowns, showing that people were living the glamorous good life."—The Times, *quoting Charles Z. Wick, a member of Mr. Reagan's Kitchen Cabinet.*

An autumn afternoon in Washington—mysterious, delirious Washington!—and all along glittering, office-lined Pennsylvania Avenue a fleet of gleaming stainless-steel buses was loading up tourists for the two-hour guided excursion of Governmentville, Image City, Tax Town, or, as it's often referred to by its residents, Our Nation's Capital. Sturdy, sweaty, plainly dressed, and somewhat pinched, the visitors from Iowa, Alabama, Vermont, Kansas, Idaho put their money down and climbed aboard— the dumpy, dull-faced folks Norma Desmond once called "those wonderful people out there in the dark." They sat down wearily and waited for a brief glimpse of the glamorous good life, a glimpse that would make their own defeated and despair-filled lives a little bit more bearable.

"See the Homes of Department Heads," the signs beside the waiting buses read. "See the Homes of Alexander Haig, Donald Regan, James Watt, William French Smith & Many Many More. See Exclusive Restaurants, Stores, Hotels, Apartment Complexes! Visit Sites of Gala Affairs. See Malt Shop Where Sandra O'Connor Was Discovered."

"Yesterday I seen William French Smith come out of a candy store," a large woman in pink stretch-pants and a "Wahoo for Washington!" T-shirt confided to a gaunt, sad-eyed woman sitting next to her on the first bus. "Wally says to me later, he says, 'Myrt, it musta been someone else,' but I knowed it was him. He was as close to me as that little gimpy guy in the cardigan up there. He give me a big smile and I about fell over. Then he got into the biggest limo you ever seen, and away he went. I'll remember that as long as I live. You know what they call him? They call him 'the Attorney General of the United States.' Ain't that beautiful?"

"You got the binocs, Myrt?" a skinny old man in the seat behind her piped up.

"In my purse," she snapped. "You can't see nothing anyway. Blind as a bat," she added, muttering to herself.

Her seatmate pulled the lever on the armrest of the reclining seat and leaned back and closed her eyes. "Me and Carl scrimped and saved for two years to come here," she said wearily. "I waitressed at the Elks Lodge on weekends, he worked nights at the worm ranch, now here we are—I can't believe it. Last night I dreamed I saw a striped tent on the White House lawn and an orchestra playing and beautiful cars parked in the driveway and women in beautiful gowns walking across the grass. I walked up to the front gate and the Secret Service said, 'Oh, hi, Mary Frances!' and I looked down and I had on a yellow chiffon gown, with rubies and emeralds and diamonds all over, and I walk in and first person I see is David Stockman. He looks at me and I look at him and I start to run and he runs after me and in the Rose Garden he grabs me and takes me in his arms and he is gasping for breath and his big eyes are looking into mine and he says, 'Don't ignore what you feel this moment! Don't pretend that you don't feel exactly what I feel! I *need* you, Mary Frances. I've wanted this all my life—your intensity, your passion, your hunger for life!' Then I woke up in the Travelodge and Carl was asleep and the TV was on. It was *him* on the TV, talking about budget cuts, just like Carl does, but it was different—it was a certain way he looked at me, a way he smiled. I don't say this to Carl, but I have strong feelings I will not be going back to Des Moines."

"Tickets, ladies?" A young man in a blue blazer was standing in the aisle next to them, with the faint trace of a smirk etched across his tanned, handsome face. He had heard some of what Mary Frances had said, and as he punched the last tickets and jumped off the bus he could hardly keep from laughing out loud.

"What's so funny, Chuck?" his friend and fellow-worker Jim asked him quizzically.

"Coupla doozies in that load," Chuck snorted. "Buncha nuts. One of 'em thinks Stockman is trying to seduce her on *Meet the Press*."

Jim turned, a faraway look in his eyes. In the distance he saw the Washington Monument beyond the White House and the Treasury. Maybe I'm crazy, too, he thought to himself.

A former campus radical, Jim had first felt drawn to Nancy Reagan in September 1980. On television, smiling and clapping for her husband, she sometimes turned and looked directly into the camera and seemed to ask Jim to come to Washington to help her and her family in an important mission that would be revealed to him later. "America is the land of promise," she seemed to say. "I want you to be very happy."

Now he and Chuck shared a studio apartment in Potomac Beach, where Jim often heard his friend, a neo-liberal, attack Washington as a city of sham, a maker of myths, a vender of illusions, and ridicule the tourists as rubes and suckers. Jim also had his doubts about the tourists—the hordes of dreary men and women with their souvenir tax-cut pens and their souvenir hats shaped like the Capitol dome, who bought issues of *Federal Romance* and *U.S. Government Confidential*, and trudged the city streets looking for the rooming house where Stockman lived when he was only a congressman, the booth at Le Bistro Louis XIV where columnist George Will holds court, the parking lot where George Bush lived (for two months in 1978) in the back seat of a 1965 Buick, when his name was Waldo Pflueger and all he had was a dream of success and a box of Ritz Crackers. There was something forlorn about it all, Jim knew, and yet whenever he walked down the Mall at night and looked across the Potomac to Arlington and saw there on the hill behind the old Lee Mansion the illuminated fifty-foot letters that spelled WASHINGTON, he felt the pull of the dream that supported his life and kept him going—the dream of becoming an Assistant Secretary of the Interior.

Interior—the very word breathed mystery, hinted at intimate secrets to be discovered, suggested the glamorous life of the

Administration insider. Jim had recently borrowed two hundred dollars from his mother, back in Topeka, to enroll in the Academy of Administration, a night school on the second floor of a dingy stucco building around the corner from Dupont Circle. Max Hugel had gone there. So had Drew Lewis, James Baker, and Edwin Meese. Every Tuesday and Thursday night, Jim attended Spokesman class, and every Wednesday night he worked with a small improvisational press-conference group in the basement of a church. On Friday nights, he took dancing lessons. One evening there, his speaking instructor took him aside. "Listen, kid," he said, putting a sympathetic arm around the young man's shoulders, "I know you think it could happen tomorrow—the call from Interior that will make all of this worth it, but, believe me, I've seen this town eat people up and spit them out. You're a nice guy. Go home, marry the girl, raise a family. Someday you'll thank me."

"I am aware that I do not speak well," Jim wrote his sweetheart that night. "But did you know that they have speechwriters here in Washington who make these big guys sound a lot smarter than they really are? Judy, I still believe that with one lucky break I can become an Assistant Secretary, right alongside James Watt, and I hope that you still believe. Someday I will send for you and we will live in a $750,000 house in Georgetown and be invited to fabulous parties. Please don't give up on me, darling, for it is your faith that gives me faith in myself."

As the tour bus rolled past the Pentagon ("The fourth-floor corner window where you see the blue satin drapes is the office of Caspar Weinberger," the bus loudspeaker blared out. "In his office Mr. Weinberger keeps more than seventy-five suits, some valued at more than one thousand dollars each, and three hundred pairs of shoes, many of them custom-made in Europe and flown to this country"), across the Potomac ("On these historic waters, members of the Cabinet frequently spend long weekends aboard their luxury yachts, some of which are up to one hundred feet in length. The President's yacht is two hundred feet in length and can remain completely submerged for up to three weeks"), and past the Lincoln Memorial ("Here, a few short weeks ago, Mr. Reagan celebrated the passage of his tax bill with a dinner party for three thousand. Marine parachutists entertained the guests with precision jumps into the Reflecting Pool, as freshman members of Congress served cold tenderloin of beef and candied carrots. The fruit salad alone came to more than six thousand dollars"), Wally and Carl stared straight ahead, stunned by the thought of the bundle this trip was costing them. Myrt and Mary Frances were planning a night on the town next, with cocktails at Nero's and dinner at the Top Hat—a blowout from which they were unlikely to escape for less than a hundred bucks per couple. Both men had hoped to return home the next morning, but now their wives were talking about renting a cab to revisit some of the high points of the bus tour. Myrt was sure she had seen Pat Buchanan peering out from the garage beside his palatial McLean, Virginia, residence, and Mary Frances had spotted a semi parked in front of the Charles Percy mansion, with "Venice Catering" emblazoned on the trailer. A man in a formal white suit was unloading crates of demitasse cups from it, using a silver forklift. Mary Frances was sure the Percys were preparing for a party, and she had a strong hunch that David Stockman would be there. "Don't laugh, Myrt, but I feel that if I could only touch him it might clear up my arthritis," she whispered.

Minutes before, riding past the vice-presidential mansion at the Naval Observatory ("Il Gazebo della Marina"), she and Myrt had pressed their faces against the window, hoping for a glimpse of George Bush. They had read his biography, *The Rest of Him:*

The George Bush Story, and loved it—the saga of an unemployed tile-setter who, while on his way to the welfare office one day, had spotted a scrap of newspaper stuffed in the coin-return of a pay telephone, unfolded it, and read that Mr. Reagan was conducting a national talent search for a Vice-President—but there was no sign of Mr. Bush in the yard now, although they did see two black Alfa-Romeos with gold trim, a large steel cage containing three ocelots, and several servants busily hanging flaming torches from the trees.

What they didn't know was that George Bush was sitting alone in the seat directly behind Wally and Carl. How could they? He was wearing dark glasses, a red wig, and a false face that had taken him three hours to apply. And yet, for George Bush, it was worth all the trouble.

He had never learned to accept the luxurious way of life of the Reagan Administration. In his heart, he was only himself, a mere tile-setter, and after all these months he still felt uneasy in his mansion, with its Moorish-style ballroom paneled in walnut and red brocade, its gold-leaf ceilings and marble floors, its terra-cotta figurines of mermaids and serpents and Egyptian deities, its grand staircase ascending to the gymnasium-sized master bedroom with the canopied bed done up to resemble a Chinese pagoda, its immense moat surrounding the mansion, its ornate Mayan lawn statuary, its giant swimming pool in the shape of the White House. No, he escaped from his new home whenever he could and mingled unnoticed among the common people. It gave him perspective, he thought, to see Washington from the outside. For a few hours now and then, he could be himself and not a glamorous figure admired by millions. "My dream is to buy a few acres in some little town where *The New York Times* isn't delivered, where 'The CBS Evening News' doesn't go, where you and I can keep a few chickens, raise vegetables, and be real people together," he had said to his wife one night on the South Portico of the White House, to which they had slipped away for a few minutes from a lavish party attended by hundreds of persons whom he had privately described as "phonies."

The bus rolled to a stop in front of Lafayette Square, and as the disguised man made his way down the aisle he was tempted momentarily to reveal himself to the two women and to take them into the White House and show them the plain truth about Washington. But no, he suddenly decided; it was far better to let them keep their dreams. Without their illusions, he thought sadly to himself, they would be utterly destroyed.

"Excuse me," Myrt said, tapping him on the arm. "Can you tell me which way is the Justice Department?"

"Sorry," he mumbled, avoiding her eyes. "I'm a stranger here myself."

There are millions of stories in Washington. These have been some of them.

Carl, *Wally*, and *Myrt* returned to Des Moines the next evening, where they continue to follow the activities of the Reagan Administration on television and in the newspapers. *Myrt* keeps a scrapbook on William French Smith.

Mary Frances remained in Washington, hoping to get a job chopping vegetables in the White House commissary. Several weeks later, she was hired as a waitress in the Senate Dining Room, where Jesse Helms, Howard Baker, and David Durenberger regularly sit in her assigned area. Through Senator Baker, she obtained a one-night waitress appointment for a gala dinner at the Reagans' ranch and was flown out to California and back. She had a color photograph taken of herself with the First Family. "The Reagans are good eaters," she wrote to *Myrt*, "but David Stockman is awful finicky. He sent his lobster back to the kitchen three times. I coulda killed him."

Chuck was discovered one day by *George Bush*, who overheard him ridicule the Republican elite and promptly hired him as a personal aide. The two often drive around the city in an old car and do ordinary things. *Mr. Bush* has been seen recently walking along the C. & O. Canal, looking at exhibits in the Smithsonian, or eating a hot dog on the south side of L Street, between Nineteenth and Twentieth.

Jim was happy for *Chuck*, and yet his friend's good fortune also depressed him, pointing up as it did his own slim prospects. One night, after writing long letters to his parents and to Judy, he took a bus to Arlington and walked up the hill through the cemetery to the base of the illuminated WASHINGTON. He climbed the "W" and stood there for a long moment, admiring the dazzling lights of the city. Then he threw himself over the edge. His fall was broken by a safety net installed there many years before, but as he landed his head hit his knee—a sharp blow, causing complete amnesia. Three days later, he was found in a pitiable condition by a wealthy Administration couple, who prefer to remain anonymous. They took him into their home, and have surrounded him with every imaginable luxury. This does not seem to have restored his faculties.

U.S. STILL ON TOP,
SAYS REST OF WORLD

"America today is Number One in the world . . ."
—PRESIDENT NIXON

The White House is very, but unofficially, elated over America's top finish in the 1971 Earth standings, announced yesterday in Geneva. The United States, for the twenty-eighth straight year, was named Number One Country by a jury of more than three hundred presidents, prime ministers, premiers, chairmen, elder world statesmen, kings, queens, emperors, popes, generalissimos, shahs, sheikhs, and tribal chieftains who hold voting membership in the Association of World Leaders.

The White House issued a brief statement acknowledging the honor and calling for "renewed dedication to the principles that have made us great," but in the West Wing, behind doors that were kept locked to reporters for forty-five minutes after the news broke, complete bedlam prevailed. Presidential assistants, special assistants, counselors, and secretaries jumped up and down and raced from suite to suite embracing each other and shouting at the tops of their voices, according to inside sources. Stacks of papers, some marked "Top Secret," were thrown from windows in jubilation, and several well-known advisers were pushed fully clothed into the showers, though not for attribution.

After a few minutes alone with Attorney General John Mitchell, President Nixon emerged from his office to address the group. His remarks were not made public by the White House, which described them as "personal in nature." The President grinned broadly and wore a wide silver-blue necktie with the inscription "El Número Uno."

With America withdrawing from a costly and divisive war abroad while beset by economic ills at home, some international observers had thought that the large Western nation might forfeit the Number One nod to the unexciting but steady Soviet Union. And when the U.S. dollar took sick a week before world leaders were to mail their ballots, it was even feared the U.S. might finish third behind the newly popular China. After the tally had been announced, however, a world leader who wished to remain anonymous said that the nearly two-hundred-year-old republic had never been in serious danger of losing the pick, at least not in leadership circles. "While some other nations have made great economic or technological strides," he remarked, "the world mantle-holder is never determined by balance sheet or record book alone. We look for basic qualities in a Number One country, such as how well it keeps its commitments, the deep spiritual resources of its people, whether or not it has been a force for peace, as well as its economic and military power per se."

It was the forty-fifth title win for the powerful industrial state since it first copped the prize in 1917. Except for some lean years in the twenties after it turned its back on the Versailles Conference, then the big-money circuit, the U.S. has dominated the world scene in this century, though it still trails the Roman and British Empires and the Mongol Horde in total wins.

In other events, China walked off with population honors, while China's Chou En-lai and Canada's Pierre Trudeau shared the Premier of the Year spotlight. The Middle East was named Foremost Trouble Spot, and in the group competition the European Community was chosen Top Bloc as well as Most Interdependent. In the small-nation runoff, honors went to Rumania (Totalitarian Division), South Korea (Free World), and India (Indies). Recognition was also given to Jordan (National Anthem), the United States (Best Credo, Most Telephones, and the G.N.P. Cup), Japan (Diplomacy, Exports, Most Benevolent Dynasty), and Micronesia (Most Trustworthy).

CONGRESS IN CRISIS:
THE PROXIMITY BILL

The Ninety-third Congress convened in January in very poor light, overshadowed as it was by the President's initiatives abroad and beset by dark omens of declining power, if not actual impotence. Among members of both parties, there was general agreement that Congress must act soon to reassert itself as a separate and equal branch of the national government, especially since congressmen found, upon opening their January pay envelopes, that an additional $25.75 had been deducted under "Misc." Calls to the Treasury Department failed to clear up the matter, largely because telephone service is so poor on the Hill. Most members have been put on party lines by a recent presidential directive aimed at curbing inflation, and telephone static is very heavy on cold days and whenever it rains.

Nowhere is the disparity of power between executive and legislative branches more evident, however, than in the area of personal inviolability. While the Presidency is whisked away to Camp David without an unfriendly eye laid on it, it isn't uncommon to see the legislative branch late at night pacing the Capitol sidewalk and calling into the darkness for a cab. The Presidency's path is cleared by squadrons of dark brown suits that carefully secure the area against perturbed or irked individuals. *Nobody* says "Hey! You!" within earshot of the Presidency. Congress walks crowded hallways and waits for elevators like the rest of us. Sometimes individuals laugh right in Congress's face. Sometimes a person yells, "Whaddaya mean, this is *your* cab? Bark off, bozo!" and almost slams the door on Congress's fingers. And every time it is jostled or its shoulder grabbed or its fingers almost pinched, a little bit of power is drained away.

The fact of legislative vulnerability was borne out dramatically on February 6, when a young man accosted Representative Frank L. Riemer (R–Cal.) in the foyer of the Rayburn Building and announced that he wanted to talk about the expanding economy and its dangerous effects on the life cycle. Rep. Riemer, whose record on environmental issues is quite good, smiled and welcomed the visitor to Washington, whereupon the youth grasped him in a bear hug and wouldn't let go. "We are one," the youth said calmly. "We embrace. We participate. We are part of each other. If one creature suffers, it must be felt by all. It is time to communicate that. It is time to go that extra mile."

With Rep. Riemer protesting strenuously, the young man then carried him outdoors, across the lawn, up the Capitol steps, and all the way to the door of the House chamber before the congressman got the attention of a guard and was let go.

Congress was naturally concerned about the incident, and a few weeks later it saw the need for new and stricter legislation when the youth was acquitted of the charge of obstructing a federal official in the performance of his duties. Defense counsel argued successfully that the accused had not obstructed the lawmaker but in fact had transported him to his place of work—a theory supported by testimony from the guard, who had heard the congressman's cry of "How dare you!" (or so Riemer testified) as a call for "More bearers!" Furthermore, defense argued, the act was not hostile but an act of love and commitment; the youth was a seminarian and presumably knew what he was doing. "His sole intent," defense stated, "was to indicate—and certainly any reasonable person would agree—that it was high time for the legislative branch to get cracking."

In directing acquittal, the trial judge complained of vagueness in the obstruction statute. "It is difficult for us under the present law as written to distinguish between actual obstruction and the perseverance of a citizen exercising his right to petition," he said, and he called on Congress to provide clearer guidelines.

The following Monday, a House Internal Security subcommittee took the matter under investigation and, to nobody's surprise, uncovered numerous instances of congressmen grasped and handled by dissident individuals. Several had been set upon by persons who, citing some moral imperative, had bound the lawmakers to themselves with twine or thread. Added to the twinings were scores of bumpings, hand-holdings, sleeve-tuggings, chest-pokings, and extremely proximitous starings and breathings. Forty-three congressmen testified or submitted affidavits, including one who recounted this episode:

> On leaving the floor to return to my office, I was aware of being followed at a close distance by a woman who seemed extremely upset. When I turned around to get a good look at her, she displayed an outstretched forefinger in a threatening manner. She closed in as we came to a group of tourists. I was then fairly certain that she intended to goose me. . . . I was caught in the crowd and couldn't get away. As I struggled across the Rotunda . . .

Thus the legislation that came to be known as the Proximity Bill began to take shape. In its first draft, it read as follows:

(1) It is the finding of Congress that Members of Congress are subject to licentious, unwarranted, and vexatious acts upon or near their persons without their consent, and that such acts do hinder, distract, or otherwise obstruct said Members from the performance of their duties.

(2) Therefore, it shall be unlawful, and punishable by a fine of not more than $1000, or imprisonment for not more than a year, or both, for any person or persons to cross state lines, or wear, display, or employ any article of clothing or any other object that has crossed state lines, to approach a Member of Congress with the thought, idea, or intention of performing said acts, including embracing, the holding of hands or other extremities, grasping of clothing, poking, pushing, lifting, or carrying, shouting at a distance of less than fifty feet, likewise singing or humming at a distance of less than ten feet, or the expulsion of breath upon said Member, or any sort of prolonged and unconsented-to proximity, whether for the purpose of portraying, communicating, or dramatizing ethical, spiritual, moral, or political principles, theories, or beliefs, or any other purpose.

Though the bill has yet to be reported out of committee, many congressmen are thought to have expressed support for it, and passage by both houses is considered not unlikely. It is felt, however, that the use of the interstate-commerce clause of the Constitution may need to be reconsidered—that the bill, as now written, leaves room for residents of the District of Columbia to perform such acts in the nude. Rep. Riemer has said that the bill should also prohibit obscene, vulgar, offensive, or "inappropriate" sounds or speech. And some congressmen are said to believe that similar protection should be granted to all citizens.

It is known that in its deliberations the subcommittee has

been looking very closely at *N.Y. Rangers* v. *Flint*, 484 F.2d
143 (11th Cir. 1971), cert. den. 415 U.S. 703 (1972). In this
case, the Eleventh Circuit Court of Appeals found that noises
made by the defendant in the direction of the Ranger goalie
were both intentional and vulgar, and, as such, tended to have
a chilling effect on his fulfillment of contractual obligations.
Setting aside the long-standing "what-kind-of-country" principle—as stated in the well-known *U.S.* v. *Heins*, 319 U.S. 626
(1943); viz., "What kind of country is this if a man can't say
what he wants?"—the court upheld the conviction. Speaking
for the majority, Judge Whirter wrote, "Nobody has the right
to act like a God-damned idiot, or to treat other people like
dirt, or to tear down all the time without having something
better to replace it with, and then come around and ask us for
favors."

RE THE TOWER PROJECT

Many of our personnel, conscious of the uncertainties of the construction business, have voiced concern relative to their future employment with the Company. What lies ahead on our horizon, they wonder, of the magnitude of the Fred M. and Ida S. Freebold Performing Arts Center, the Tannersfield Freeway Overpass, and other works that have put us in the construction forefront? They recall the cancellation in mid-contract of the Vietnam Parking Lot project, and they ask, "Will the Super-Tall Tower project, too, go down the drain, with a resultant loss of jobs and Company position in the building field?"

The Company believes such will not be the case. While we aren't putting all our "eggs" on one tower and are keeping an eye on the Los Angeles–Honolulu Bridge option and the proposed Lake Michigan Floating Airport, we feel that the Super-Tall Tower has achieved priority status in Washington, and all phases of research and development, land clearance, and counter-resistance are moving forward in expectation of final approval.

As for the Tower critics, they are few in number, and there isn't one of their objections that we haven't answered. Let's look at the record. Their favorite line is "Why build a Super-Tall Tower when money is so urgently needed for cancer and poverty?" With all due respect to the unwell or impoverished person and his or her family, we state our case as follows:

First, Tower construction will create a hundred thousand new jobs, not only in the Babel area and the Greater Southwest but also in other places where the bricks and slime will be made by subcontractors.

Second, because it will be the world's tallest tower, we will be able to see more from it than from any existing tower.

Third, we have reason to believe the Chinese are well along in the development of *their* tower. If we don't wish to abdicate tower leadership to Communist nations, however friendly at the moment, we can't afford to slow down now. To do so would mean the waste of all the money spent on tower research so far and would set back American tower technology for decades to come. Thus, our national prestige is at stake—not merely national pride but the confidence in our ability to rise toward the heavens. When a nation turns away from the sky and looks at its feet, it begins to die as a civilization. Man has long dreamed of building a tall tower from which he could look out and see many interesting and unusual things. Most Americans, we believe, share this dream.

Fourth, environmentalist groups have predicted various disastrous effects from the Tower—that the humming noise of its high-speed elevator will be "unbearable" to the passengers and to nearby residents, that its height will confuse migrating birds, that its long shadow will anger the sun, and so forth. The Company's research laboratory has engaged in a crash program that has already achieved a significant degree of hum reduction; at the same time, our engineers are quick to point out that since no elevator now in service can approach the speed and accompanying hum projected for the Tower elevator, there is no viable data on which to base the entire concept of an "unbearable" hum. Such a determination must wait until the completion of the Tower. In any event, the hum may serve to warn off approaching birds. As for the sun, we feel that, with certain sacrifices, this problem can be taken care of.

HOW IT WAS IN AMERICA
A WEEK AGO TUESDAY

A couple of us were sitting around in the United States of America one night not long ago when we got this idea for a magazine article. We would call up housewives, farmers, doctors, white-collar workers, black people, students, town officials, teachers, urban planners, airline spokesmen, White House sources, leading economists, cabdrivers, newspaper editors, environmental experts, ministers, controversial writers, moderate Republicans, telephone operators, mediators, welfare recipients, observers, low-income families, grain brokers, country-and-western singers, skilled craftsmen, motorists, steelworkers, rural Americans, alternative life-stylists, bystanders, commuters, historians, gay persons, investors, and small children in California, Louisiana, Toledo, the Apostle Islands, San Jose, Syracuse, Cook County, the Great Plains, Poughkeepsie, New Jersey, North Dakota, Dallas, Duluth, Orlando, Knoxville, New York City,

Wichita, Washington, D.C., Winnetka, Kennebunkport, Key Largo, Omaha, Amarillo, Ohio, Oklahoma, Amherst, Tallahassee, Tennessee, and East St. Louis, and ask, "How's it going?" Then we would write the article.

All too often, we felt, the media are guilty of reporting the "big" stories and completely overlooking what it's all about—what people are up to and how it looks to them, the constant ebb and flow and pace and rhythm and ceaseless change of our lives, and more or less just what it's like to live in America today and have problems and hopes and fears and dreams and to go to work and come home and watch TV or go to a show or maybe just settle down with a good book or an in-depth magazine article.

Of course, we are all guilty of this to some extent. We tend to think of days as being rather similar to each other, except maybe Christmas, or New Year's, or Saturday. However, as the editors of the *Life* Special Report on "One Day in the Life of America" wrote recently, "Days are like fingerprints, no one exactly like another in its whorls and ridges." Or, one might say, like magazine articles, each with its quite different paragraphs and neatly printed but various hundreds of words, many of them verbs.

Some people, in fact, may consider our project rather similar to the *Life* Special Report. But they are as different as two sunrises, or billfolds, or yesterday and tomorrow, or Oakland and Chicago avenues in Minneapolis.

Hours before the sun, its rays racing westward at the speed of light, its estimated 267 tints dancing on the choppy, oil-streaked waters of the Atlantic, rose, Earth had turned the United States of America, time zone by time zone, into a Tuesday in midwinter. For most Americans, it came in their sleep in the middle of the night, marked by only a barely perceptible change in rapid eye movements, a slight shifting of position in bed. Their attitudes toward Tuesday were yet vague, uncomprehending. Awakened by telephone calls, they tended to feel it was something they could put off until morning.

Even as America slept, West Germany and the Soviet Union had forged ahead in Tuesday production, and Japan was going home to rest up for Wednesday. In a darkened Labor Department, at Fourteenth and Constitution in Washington, figures sheathed in Manila folders spelled out in eight-point type growing unemployment and spiraling inflation.

If there were fears or hopes among friends and foes that America might not get out of bed this morning, however, they were quickly dispelled. Already, the first of 125 million beds, 160 million cigarettes, and 40 million quarts of orange juice were creaking, smoking, and being poured. Four hundred million socks lay in sock drawers waiting to be worn, the holes in them totaling 700,000 square feet, almost as large as the White House grounds.

In the dim light of the Executive Bedroom, the 64-percent–approved President was assessing his own sock options. A few minutes before, in keeping with presidential tradition, he had pulled on his pants one leg at a time, and now, donning a pair of wool sweat socks first worn by former President Eisenhower, he slipped into black hightop shoes from the Hoover Administration and made his way along a darkened corridor toward the Toaster Room.

As daylight spread over the populous, historic East to the fertile Midwest, far-flung Plains, scenic Mountain, and booming Pacific regions, lights came on in millions of homes, apartments, condominiums, town houses, duplexes, mobile homes, hospitals, halfway houses, and correctional institutions. Throats were cleared, toothpaste tubes squeezed, doors slammed, and long strips of bacon arrayed on pans to crackle over low-to-moderate heat. Women sighed, brushed their hair, scolded children, flipped pancakes, tied shoelaces. Men gulped coffee, scanned headlines, put on coats, started cars. Children whimpered, watched TV cartoons, kicked each other, left crusts, wheedled small change. Millions of dogs dozed in breakfast nooks or wandered aimlessly into living rooms.

In Eastport, Maine, the easternmost restaurant owner in the country, Buford Knapp, paused between orders of eggs and hashbrowns to raise his prices another nickel. Residents of the Gabriel Nursing Home in Minneapolis were wheeled to their windows for the flag-raising and pledge of allegiance. A bus rumbled along historic Market Street in San Francisco. A flock of bluebirds described graceful arcs over downtown Knoxville.

In the kitchen of a farm commune near Middlebury, Vermont, Norman Lefko slid a pan of blueberry muffins into the ancient wood stove and sat down at a plant table to read the Sunday *New York Times*. In New York, Craig Claiborne arose briefly for a glass of tomato juice. As he did so, Fargo housewife Eula Larpenteur prepared fried eggs, following Claiborne's own recipe ("Break the desired number of eggs into a saucer and slip them carefully into the pan. . . . If the eggs are to be cooked on both sides, turn with a pancake turner") and listening to "Don't Give Me a Drink," the new Carson Trucks hit. Meanwhile, Carson Trucks slept fitfully in the Cartesian Suite of the Mambo Motel in Shreveport, having played to an overflow crowd in the Memorial Auditorium the night before. At that moment, "Don't Give Me a Drink" was being heard in St. Louis, Orlando, Wichita, and Philadelphia (where baseballer Pete Rose had just nicked his cheek). It was not being heard in Chicago, where columnist Ann Landers was reading her first letter of the day. "Dear Ann," it began. "The woman who said she was tired of her husband's snoring made me sick to my stomach. . . ."

And so the morning began. For several hours, time seemed

to pass quickly. Before Americans knew it, it was almost noon Eastern Standard Time. They had worked hard, the more than 77 million employed in mining, construction, manufacturing, transportation, sales, finance, personal services, and government, and now it was time for lunch. They had earned it. Although $1.75 billion of debt had been incurred, 124 persons killed on highways, and $8 million more spent on cigarettes than on education, $2 billion had been added to the gross national product that Tuesday morning. Steel had been rolled, buses driven, beds made, reports typed, tape recorders assembled, Shakespeare taught, windows wiped, washing machines repaired, major policy changes announced. Now the first of 4.6 million cans of soup were opened, the last of 2 million plates of leftovers were brought out of refrigerators. Waxed paper crackled in crowded lunchrooms, waitresses from Miami to Seattle yelled, "One with, skip the pickle," and a gigantic tidal wave of egg salad, tuna, and peanut butter was spread over 89 million slices of bread. Among those who did not eat lunch were Baba Ram Dass, Seiji Ozawa, Francis Tarkenton, and Selby Dale, a stockbroker in San Diego. The Dow-Jones industrial average was down eight points at noon, and his breakfast had come up at eleven.

As the nation slipped into afternoon, it seemed to lose stride and falter. Clocks were watched, wheels spun. From the sequoia-shaded Pacific Coast to the stubbled Kansas wheat fields to rockbound Maine, the national mood shifted to one of boredom, then apathy and resignation, with an occasional moment of outright despair. Many, it is true, maintained momentum. The President, meeting with his economic advisers, pledged continued efforts to curb inflation. The Secretary of State, speaking at the National Press Club, called for continued efforts to establish structures for peace. Hundreds of other efforts continued, or were pledged or called for, as did numerous operations, campaigns, programs, and attempts. Talks on new contracts continued. Searches for lost persons continued, and hopes remained high. Wars against cancer, school dropouts, crime, unemployment, pollution, and discrimination went on, along with planning for the coming biennium, Middle East peace talks, *The Fantasticks*, and scores of investigations. Hearings resumed. Many ends, or the beginnings of ends, were sighted.

Nonetheless, interest, for the most part, lagged. Polls showed a 25 percent jump in indecision after lunch: "Don't know" was up almost a third; "Don't care one way or the other" and "Both are just as bad" showed similar increases. In New Haven, sophomore Raymond Doswell took ten minutes to remember the composition of methane. In Albuquerque, New Mexico, Ernest Hollard, a thirty-two-year-old architect, lost the will to live. (Fortunately, nothing was wrong with him, and he soon felt cheerful enough to sharpen several pencils.) In Fargo, Eula Larpenteur called a local radio station and requested anything by the Chenilles. Henny Youngman spoke to a luncheon in Des Moines and made a joke about small businessmen. In hospitals around the country, thousands were treated for self-inflicted cuts suffered in moments of inattention. An estimated 40,000 lost faith in the political process, even though, as of midafternoon, it remained strong and viable. In Shreveport, Carson Trucks abused a bottle of cough syrup.

Many people knew it. Others wondered what it was. Some mistook it for something else. In New York, however, eating sautéed carrots boiled to extinction, Craig Claiborne knew it. John Simon knew it, and knew that he knew it. So did cabdriver Jack Poderhotz. ("People are sheer stark raving crazy nuts. Quote me.") In Colorado, author (*Fear and Loathing*) Hunter S. Thompson knew it. The big mudslide has started, he thought while writing. This is it. Giant hair balls roll westward, barbiturates float in the reservoirs. Merv smiles on television. The country bleeds from the gums, walks straight into trees.

Of the 6,554 luncheon audiences addressed today, most were told not to sell short. Now, a scant two hours later, the country seemed less sure of itself and its destiny, values, strength, role in the free world, commitment to the arts, and the basic worth of its younger generation, most of whom were in school and, in turn, didn't care for it, if Janice Hoyt of Boise was typical. She thought it reeked.

In Washington, several high-ranking congressional sources felt a sudden wave of intense personal disgust. Journalist Robert Sherrill wadded up a sheet of blank paper and threw it angrily at a potted culp. Eight news conferences were canceled for no reason, including one with a farm spokesman, who had planned to display a hamburger bun and then reveal the few small crumbs of it that are the farmer's portion. Midway through his Chicago radio show, Studs Terkel—talking about the human spirit, the young, Joe Hill, Bach, Lady Day, the life urge, the "little man," Chaplin, the sea, and (his guest on the show) Phil Donahue—faltered, said "But of course that's only my opinion. Others may feel differently," and went to a commercial for patio furniture, causing several Evanston listeners to look out across Lake Michigan for a long time. Eagles were observed diving beak first into the frozen Mississippi north of Brainerd, Minnesota. Strange grinding noises over the horizon were heard by crews of oil tankers in the Gulf of Mexico.

As the sun swept westward toward the Far East, as long shadows fell, from the oyster beds of Maryland to Houston's Astrodome to Seattle's Puget Sound, few Americans took umbrage at the passing of the day, and regret was felt by few of the millions who clogged freeways, jostled on trains and subways, jammed buses, piled into taxis, hopped on bicycles, or took off on foot for the 2.6-mile average trip home. At colleges around the country, suggested reading lists of books for further enrichment were stuffed in wastebaskets, and only 86 students remained after class for personal help. The Boston Bruins ended practice early. At the Purity Packing Plant, in Louisville, two workers scrawled obscenities on a hog carcass. In the Oval Office, the President looked at the last item on his schedule ("Call AFL-CIO—ask labor's coop in days, weeks ahead"), said "The hell with it," and went upstairs to toss quoits. In the garden outside his window, a White House guard spat into a rosebush, chucked a rock at a sparrow. At the State Department, the search for lasting peace slowly wound down, ending officially at 7:40, when the Secretary was logged out of his office, trailed by his bodyguard, Knute. His mind, accustomed to penetrate far beyond the limits of normal men's endurance, had begun to lag shortly after six. Left behind on his desk were four legal-size papers filled with doodled sketches of horses, slippers, obelisks, holsters, curtains, and peninsulas.

As his limousine sped away from the government curb, Mrs. Buford Knapp was putting on a Polynesian beach dress and coral accessories for a luau at the Eastport V.F.W.; Norman Lefko was carving a handmade maple-syrup ladle; Eula Larpenteur was telling her husband, Stanley, to take it easy on their oldest son, Craig, sixteen, who was expected home momentarily from a brush with the law. Elsewhere, millions prepared for the evening. Tons of macaroni-and-cheese casseroles baked slowly in moderate heat, hundreds of square miles of tablecloth were smoothed out, and an estimated 45,000 women discovered, to their mild surprise, unsightly spots on glasses and dinnerware. Newspapers were opened, legs were crossed, and alcohol was consumed—enough to carry Bismarck, North Dakota, through the seven-month home-heating season.

At night, America becomes a study in contrasts between light and darkness. This night was no exception. Street lights in cities, villages, townships twinkled in the cold winter air. Neon signs flashed their potpourri of messages. The lights in houses cast bright rectangular shapes onto snowy lawns and sidewalks.

Car headlights made fascinating patterns, delicate traceries captured by hundreds of amateur photographers at slow shutter speeds. Traffic lights blinked red and green, as did the lights of aircraft, radio and television towers, police cars and other emergency vehicles, and hundreds of miles of unnoticed Christmas lights remaining on trees or outlining front porches.

At NBC master control in New York, technical difficulties produced a momentary blurring of John Chancellor, prompting 17.5 million persons to lean forward and adjust their sets—an outlay of energy equivalent to 4,000 barrels of crude oil. A majority of Americans would spend at least part of the evening watching television, of which a small minority (28 percent) would fall asleep while doing so. Others looked forward to movies, plays, ballets, concerts, or intimate dinner parties, for which women sat before mirrors making expressive faces and applying cosmetics, and spent an accumulated national total of almost 400 woman-years, or a lot longer than the Ming Dynasty. Meanwhile, men ran a Niagara of hot water into bathtubs and showers and shaved an area the size of the Pentagon.

Of the 3.5 million Americans who went "out" for the evening, many had a good time, despite the dimly remembered uneasiness of the afternoon, while for countless others it was "O.K." or "not bad." Very few experienced real bummers. Those who did included Buford Knapp, who was publicly berated by his wife for not sending the clams back to the kitchen. She said there was dirt in them. Forty-five cultural events received poor reviews, including three Beethoven Sixth Symphonies ("An exercise in pointlessness," "A leaden sense of rhythm," and "If this is pastoral, then what is sheer tedium?," respectively), and roughly half of the evening's sporting events were lost by one team or the other.

Winning or losing, at home or away, shirts or skins, most Americans found some pleasure before midnight and retired at a reasonable hour to sleep for slightly less than eight hours (Tuesday night is the most restful night in the country—Saturday is the least, leading Sunday afternoon by only two hours—although urban sleepers do slightly better on Wednesday) and to dream, if a test group at U.C.L.A. was indicative, about familiar scenes and faces.

Not that there weren't disturbing signs to upset even the most complacent. In New York, hours after the market had closed, the Dow-Jones industrial average dropped three points unnoticed. In Dallas, a four-year-old child suddenly spoke in her sleep words of dire warning to her parents and to all Americans. And two women sitting in a back yard in Key West, Florida, observed a large, vacuum-cleaner–shaped object with flashing blue lights hover and then land fifty feet away, beside a garage. Two persons in yellow raincoats emerged, exposed themselves briefly, got back in the craft, and flew away. The craft emitted a low hum, like a dial tone. The persons appeared to be from another planet entirely.

If all was not well, it was nevertheless mostly pretty good, on balance. Despite its problems, the nation slipped into a fundamentally sound sleep. Many Americans tossed in their beds, got up to pace the floor, took aspirin, were troubled, pondered complex matters, stared at ceilings, but this was by no means common. And even the restless, for the most part, slept. From the vast bedroom suburbs of New Jersey to sleepy river towns in Minnesota to the long-slumbering natural resources of Alaska, America slept. It slept because it was tired. Soon it was midnight, and another day (and another magazine article) was over.

MISSION TO MANDALA

In last month's issue of *First Brigade*, we saw Joe and Jim launch the flying skiff *Capability* from the U.S.S. *Enterprise*, Floating HQ of the famous First, and set course for Mandala, mysterious island stronghold of the treacherous Celanese. Hours passed. To anxious buddies waiting for word—Rocco, Izzy, Chief Thunder, Mojo, Mike, Captain O'Connor, Nurse Nancy—they seemed like days. "*Mama mia!* It's-a no use-a," said Rocco, manning the scanner that was fine-tuned to pick up faint flickers from Joe and Jim's solar-powered laser signal rings. "Keep trying, Rock!" muttered Captain O'Connor grimly. "I know the boys are trying to get through to us—I just know it!" Suddenly, Izzy heard taps on his headset. "*Oy veh,*" he sighed. "If it's bed news you vant, Keptain, boy, hef I got da bed news!" Faithful to their orders, the two youths had maintained radio silence, but by tapping on solid subterranean surfaces they had managed to send a Morse-code message by way of the Brigade's highly sensitive seismograph, informing HQ that they were trapped in an abandoned mine shaft and hopelessly surrounded by screaming Celanese terrorists crazed by anti-American rhetoric and dominated by their Cuban Communist mercenary masters! On the decks of the *Enterprise*, initial dismay and disbelief were quickly replaced by quiet determination as the ship swung hard to starboard. Communications Control crackled with crisp orders. "Them little gimps think America says 'uncle,' I reckon it's up to us to give 'em a lesson in *English*," Mike said confidently. "C'mon, Marie and Louise," Mojo whispered to his fists. "Time for you to do the *talkin'*."

Can the First do the job? Can a New York City cabdriver, an ex–welterweight champ, a San Francisco short-order cook, a Nebraska farm boy, a direct descendant of Crazy Horse, a former tailback for the Fighting Irish, and the first woman to perform successfully an arterial bypass on a mountaintop in a blizzard— can a crack team of diehard individuals intervene and, with minimal loss of human life, rescue Joe and Jim—a veteran C.I.A. operative and an A.D.A. vice-president who loves opera? Or does Mandala mean curtains? Is it time to turn tail, run up the white flag, call off the dogs, and generally cheese it? Is it time to cash in Old Glory?

More from Mandala in a minute. First, this month's mailbag:

Here's a big salute to all you guys at Able Baker Comics, especially the artists. Jerry's work on the preventive air strike in the November ish was superb—great action, beautiful color! Just one complaint. How could Joe and Jim walk into an abandoned mine shaft? It has "TRAP" written all over it. These guys are supposedly trained in anti-terrorist tactics (A.T.T.), but sometimes they don't have the smarts to dial Information. Did they eat Dumb Flakes for breakfast? C'mon! Let's get both oars in the water!

L.F., NEW HAVEN

A low blow, L.F., and it hurts, man, no lie. You're calling two guys dumb who rigged up a makeshift bombsight from a beer bottle and a mess kit when the *Capability* came through Chinese ack-ack looking like Swiss cheese and planted 500-pounders in Mao's chow mein, giving Chiang Kai-shek time to reach Taiwan ("Yanks Over Yangtze")? You say two soldiers are stupid who snuck behind V.C. lines, disguising themselves by squinting, and blazed a fake Ho Chi Minh Trail that led two thousand N.V.D. regulars straight into the arms of the Third Division ("Tête-à-Tet")? It's armchair commanders like you, L.F., who make fighting for democracy the thankless job that it is. Glad you liked November's art, though. We plan more preventive air strikes in the very near future, so be on the lookout.

I have every Able Baker comic going back to 1942. *First Brigade* is tops in my book, followed by *Screaming Leathernecks, Charlie Squadron, Still Subs Run Deep, Slim Smith—Secret Agent, Battling Seabees, Defense Plant Workers in War and Peace,* and *Wally Randolph—Air Raid Warden,* in that order. One question—

Fire away.

In Vol. IV, No. 8, after witnessing the Japanese surrender, Joe plans to return to Middleburg and become an inventor. In Vol. XII, No. 4, at Panmunjom, Jim asks Sgt. Monica York to marry him. In more recent issues, the boys frequently mention wanting to settle down Stateside. Now, trapped in the mine shaft, Jim says he'd give anything for a Coke and a cheeseburger. Are these hints of upcoming retirement, possibly of disbanding the entire Brigade?

B.D., SAN LUIS OBISPO

Not on your ever-lovin' life, B.D. That question was answered once and for all when carrier-based Zeros approached Oahu one quiet Sunday morning years ago. When word was flashed to the U.S. of A., Joe was in his garage-workshop, attaching airbrakes with C-clamps to his landau, and Jim was listening to Act III of *Aïda*. They left home and never looked back. Sure, they miss it—Mom, Bud, Sis, the shady streets, Sunday dinner, swimming in the Mississippi, the sweet smell of sassafras, sarsaparilla, and blackstrap molasses—but don't mistake homesickness for lack of resolve. Joe and Jim intend to stay up front for as long as it takes. Why? Check your back yard. See enemy troops digging foxholes in the sandbox? No? Good. Let's keep it that way.

I wish that *First Brigade* could be read in every college classroom in America. Maybe it would show today's generation that a volunteer army is an army only if people volunteer. It's up to them. Why is it we always run when we should do what must be done? We'd always rather joke and kid and talk about the things we did, or fret and worry, moan and stew, than tackle the job that's ours to do. If Americans would only fight for everything we know is right, we soon would have a better life free of suffering and strife.

D.M., OMAHA

Consider the nail hit on the head, D.M. Wake up and smell the coffee, students.

The First Brigade is great, especially Mojo and Chief Thunder. Good to see members of so-called "minority" groups who are willing to fight for the land they love. My only complaint has to do with smoking. I know Captain O'Connor is under a great deal of pressure, but it makes me sick to see cigarettes dangling from his lips. Cigarettes sap a person's vital resources. It's just plain wrong to show them as a sign of manliness.

B.T., ORLANDO

Good point, B.T., and we'll pass it on. A word to the wise should be sufficient. Meanwhile, let's not forget "Allies über Alles" when the Captain lobbed a Zippo into the Nazi fuel dump, or the exploding cigar in "A Gift for Göring."

The Mandala crisis puts me in mind of two similar adventures. In 1942, trapped in a deep bunker on Corregidor, Joe and Jim fasted forty days until, thin enough to wriggle up the secret airshaft, they escaped the Imperial Japanese Army and reached the open Pacific in time to guide MacArthur's landing boats through mine-infested waters. In 1966, trapped in a Viet Cong cave beneath Hill 109, Joe and Jim called in an air strike right on top of them, and the Air Force, in a textbook display of precision bombing, hit the geological fault right on the money, surgically splitting open the hill and enabling the boys to climb out and be rescued by commandos. I'm confident the First will find a way this time too. Just one little quibble: when the Celanese attack the mouth of the mine shaft, you have their SM-82s going "BLAM-BLAAAMMM." According to the latest *Jane's Guns*, that would be "RA-A-A-A-T-RA-A-A-A-A-T." Keep up the good work.

M.G., PHOENIX

Our faces are red, M.G. We confused the SM-82 with the C-24. Your vigilance gives Joe and Jim an even better chance of surviving the attack until the First arrives—as you know, the SM-82 lacks the anti-rock capability of the C-24. Precious minutes have been won. Accept our thanks.

A few years ago, in the Mayaguez incident, Joe and Jim employed stink bombs to render enemy forces helpless with disgust. Now here they are trapped in a mine shaft where stink bombs would be highly effective and on page 24 Joe even points out to Jim that Celanese can't wear gas masks because their heads are too small—but where are the bombs??? What gives? Don't go barefoot to a snake-stomping, as my Dad used to say. Did the guys just plain forget them or what?

G.E., NASHVILLE

Hold on there, G.E. Don't run off half-cocked. Stink bombs come under chemical warfare, and thanks to bleeding hearts in Washington, these valuable tools have been taken out of the hands of the First Brigade. So don't complain to us. Write your Congressman.

Now back to our story.

Deep beneath Mandala, dodging Celanese shells that ricocheted off the mine-shaft walls (BLAAANGG! KA-CHINGGG!) and hand grenades bouncing down the steeply slanted floor (THUNK-THUNK-THUNK-THUNK-THUNK-THUNK-BLAAAAMMMMM!!), armed only with M-16s (KRRAKK! KRRAKK!), a flame-thrower (KER-WHOOOOSHHHH!), and a bullhorn (WE HAVE JUST ONE RESPONSE-ONSE-ONSE-ONSE . . . TO YOUR DEMAND FOR SURRENDER-ER-ER-ER; NUTS!-TS!-TS!-TS!), Joe and Jim crouched behind a large rock, which Celanese firepower was slowly making smaller and smaller. "Where in blazes is the First?" Jim shouted over the din. "Sometimes—sometimes I get the feeling—oh, never mind," he murmured.

"What??!! Get *what* feeling??!!" Joe answered. Twenty-seven years spent crouched next to Jim in one hellhole after another had made him sensitive to the feelings of his younger partner, a liberal and a graduate of a small liberal-arts college, who, unlike Joe—who, like most men of scientific bent, expressed himself plainly and forthrightly—often hesitated and had to be coaxed.

"Sometimes I get the feeling the First is only symbolic," said Jim. "Ever-present—sure! but symbolism all the same."

Joe's eyes rolled up in his smoke-blackened face. He sighed wearily, lighting his last cigarette as he did so. Although he knew that he could always count on the young activist when the chips were down, he had long since come to distrust Jim's doubts, his ever-present skepticism, not to mention his tendency, common among liberals, to want to get into long discussions just when it's time to hunker down and aim for the eyeballs.

"Listen," he rasped. "H_2O is a symbol too. Does that mean you don't believe in water?" He paused, hoping the message would sink in, when suddenly Jim grabbed him.

"That's it!" Jim yelled. "Listen!"

From a narrow crevice beneath their feet came the unmistakable sound of running water. "It's an underground river," said Jim. "Smells like fresh water. That means it runs *to* the sea."

Joe smiled. "See if you can squeeze through that crevice," he said. "I'll hold 'em off."

Meanwhile, aboard the *Enterprise*, Captain O'Connor awaited the arrival of powerful magnets from Midway Island, magnets that, according to physicists, could be mounted in the bellies of low-flying B-52s, yanking the little heads of the Celanese up by the chin-straps of their iron helmets and preventing them from aiming accurately at Joe and Jim as the boys fled from the mine shaft. It had been Nurse Nancy's idea—a whiplash attack—and she watched the Captain anxiously now as he paced the windswept deck. "How much longer can he go on like this?" she asked herself, silently. "The aneurysm is as big as a fist. How can I tell him?" Unaware of her, unaware that Joe and Jim had been carried from Mandala by the underground river and even now were swimming hand over fist in the wrong direction against powerful waves dotted with the fins of killer sharks, he strode back and forth, his eyes fixed eastward, exhaling through his nostrils.

NANA HAMI BA REBA

I had just motored the night shield over the dome and coordinated into the body pod to initiate sleep mode when the Chief Exec's audible crackled over the talk circuit embedded in my third upper-left molar. "Curt," it snapped. "Meeting in fifteen seconds in the Nute. I'll send a ray."

"Mmm," I said, "Mmm-hmm." I removed the foam pad I keep in my mouth at night to prevent teeth-grinding. I was already up and pulling a clean shirt from the dispenser. *Fifteen seconds!* Then my memory clicked in.

I lived forty years under Old Time, and long after metrification I still hadn't adjusted and sometimes took several rems to work out the Old Time equivalent. The hardest unit for me was the New Second, or centi-while, which equals 86.4 Old Seconds, the O.S. having become the rem, or "twinkling of the eye" (tote). I was the only person in Long-Range Linguistics not wearing a digital watch, and the C.E. kept nominating to me as "one of the Old Hands" and would often quest, "What time is it?" hoping to catch me off-digital—hoping I'd read, "Oh, about quarter of eight" or "A little past noon."

It was two-ninety-six when I pulled on my pants. I stepped into the wave, particularized my face and hands, and brushed my teeth with salt. (I had a high-frequency dentalaxis, but it reminded me of a teething ring; besides, it didn't do a thing for the gums.) I tried to pre-think what the meeting would be in re (time? space? some continuum of both?), who would exist at it, whether my job was on the spectrum. Most of all, or 98 percent, I hoped the C.E. would not send a ray.

Rays had been a big item with him since his election—Number Four on his ten-point program, the Big Rush, which overwhelmed his opponent (CBS declared him six totes after the board closed) and swept him into the Preemy Gaga. Of course, total metrification (weight, space, time, language) was Number One, and for that I accept a measure of guilt.

Six months (O.T.) before he was declared, I published a book, *The Crisis* (still available in video chip), which read that the energy shortage (the crisis in the title) represented only a shortage of will and imagination, a momentary setback before the breakthrough, a brief commercial for despair before the scenario resumed. It was then almost 1984 (O.T.), four digits that, owing to George Arliss's book, were embedded in the national mind as the date of totalitarian onset, and productivity was declining and suspicion mounting as people turned inward. "We need a breakthrough," I output. "People are down on America. We need to change their minds." I thought metric could stop the drop and start the upturn.

The C.E. bought it (and, later, me). The Big Rush promised metric. It promised spin-offs and trade-ins. It promised every New Trend, Coming Thing, and Major Development that magazine writers had been touting for twenty years: cable-television sets with eighty channels that also retrieve information, pay bills, and make coffee; plus monorails, PicturePhones, Copter-Cars, disposable clothes, bubble-top homes, and everything else you used to see in *Boys' Life, Popular Science,* and the Sunday *Chronicle* rotogravure under the title "What the World Will Be Like in 1970."

As it turned out, of course, 1984 became a stepping stone, not a stumbling block—to use a phrase the C.E. used to like before he went to visuals. Everything changed completely, and I got a low-lying job in Linguistics verbalizing nouns, etc. "Language lags. Make updates. New it," the C.E. sentenced. (Or, in Metro, "Swakfon na wah to neba. Dit. Moto.") It wasn't a bad job. Mostly, I sat around relapsing and playing with UniSam, a DadaBan 2000.

"HELLO HOW ARE YOU?" it keyed when I turned it on.

"SAM YOU MADE THE PANTS TOO LONG," I quipped.

Two rems later, it read me a national inseam analysis, trending possible seat-sag and crotch-drop curves and fixing coordinates of cuff-collapse. "WHO SAM?" it queried. "FIRST ONE TO TALK IS A MONKEY'S UNCLE," I replied, and back came a readout on the ancestry of every male primate in America and the line, "WHO FIRST?"

"WHO'S ON SECOND?" I gagged.

Much as I enjoyed computers, rays were another matter. I had a ray pad in my bay, and it terrified me to step on it and be instantly materialized to a destination. "Lasers are safe. Kaba anoka" was the slogan of PopComm, which ran the rays, but they couldn't seem to iron out the wrinkles. PopComm included a good many executives from the old Amtrak, and just as in the Old Days, time was immaterial to them. You might wait for hours to be materialized and then be materialized into an alien sector, there to wait on hold for prioritizing; meantime you could have called a cab and been on-site and back and debriefed and in the pod. Sometimes you would not be materialized at all. Sometimes you would be materialized but not your pants. Sometimes you would be pre-materialized, or backflashed—a ray malfunction known as a "retro," which, though uncommon, had materialized more than a few passengers into vaudeville, Canada, Reo roadsters, or Methodist theology.

Three-ten: I had been in the Nute often, but it never ceased to amaze me. Although on the surface it resembled an ordinary nutrition bay in any American home, the Nute was dissimulated, differential. The microwave could send a favorite dish anywhere in the world, also recept. The compactor reduced nonessentials to nothing. The blender could not only blend but also meld, mix, mingle, and associate. With its gleaming formats, and with the quotients and coefficients humming and the programs on the back burner, the Nute was a model of maximization. No wonder the C.E. liked to say, "If you can't execute, get out of the Nute."

Now, however, he was saying, "Fremser. Fremser gana reno." As I did so, a tube emerged from the format and juiced me.

"Qataba no nee. Baba freem ba la bana. Luru wana to muni. Gogi baba ga tanda so nina fron."

Well-versified though I am in Metro—a language superior to English and more easily understood because it uniforms spelling and pronunciation, activates the passive, presents the past, subjects the verb, and singles meanings—I was stumped. Looped. *Baba freem ba la bana?*

"Nubi gana, bwana. Weeni lala," I stammered. ("I am not impacted by that which you have spoken. The number you have reached is not a working number." At least, that's what I meant, although I was occurred to that I might have said that the elk were upwind of the river.

He sighed and drummed his fingers as he visualized me

impatiently. He had always been impatient with those who could not keep up. After years of speaking English, some of us were accustomed to looking up strange words in Western's, but Metro had no Western's, of course, because it changed so rapidly. And the C.E.'s daily update chips gave no English equivalent for new modes and phrases. "Metro cannot *be* equaled," he often stated. "It does not translate, it separates. Think Metro on its own terms. Don't relate it—*resonate.*"

"Lana guru ma soni. Baba lu a runi," he said wearily. Then, slowly and irrationally, tilting forward and depressing his voice level so as not to trip the light on the warning board, he told me in plain English that my number was up.

I had enemies, he related—dozens of them—who were on him like a ton of bricks demanding a pound of flesh, and although he was willing to go the second mile, government was a game of inches, and an ounce of prevention was worth a pound of cure. He was going to have to deep-six me. Terminate me with favor. A retro, in other words. I would be materialized out to pasture. The back forty. The hinter hectares.

"Nana hami ba reba," he murmured. "Nu?"

I stood up. How could I say "Nu" to my Chief Executive? With an empty heart, I worded in the affirmative.

"Is it safe to go back?" I asked. ("Olli olli infree?")

"Doni hemo ba sumo," he answered.

I will always be deeply gratified that he removed himself at this point, to allow my last moments in the future to have been private and self-oriented before my being retroed to a time in the past that I was then unable to have remembered.

I was to take a last look at the Nute and all it will stand for, the world I will help to make, and then, with fond and positive memories of the future, I was to take the final step and place myself upon the ray pad and be output.

I had just stepped on the pad and closed my eyes when I

heard the shrill voice of a young boy as he came bounding down the stairs. "Hi, Dad! Hi, Mom!" he yelled. "What's for supper?"

"Meat and potatoes," I heard myself saying. "Wash up, son. Dinner's on the table in fifteen minutes."

"O.K., Dad!" he cried. "Where's David?"

"Hey, let's keep it down to a dull roar," I said. "First things first. What'd you learn in school today?"

"Nuthin'," he said.

4

MY STEPMOTHER, MYSELF

Recently in Weeseville, Pennsylvania, a woman was dismissed from her job as a human-resources coordinator and driven over a cliff by an angry mob of villagers carrying flaming torches and hurling sharp rocks after they learned that she was married to a man who had custody of his three children by a previous marriage.

In California, soon after her marriage to a prince (her first marriage, his seventh), a woman named Sharon Mittel was shut up in a dungeon under the provisions of that state's Cruel and Unnatural Parent Act, which allows the immediate imprisonment of a stepparent upon the complaint of a stepchild. The prince's oldest daughter accused Sharon of slapping her. She was later freed after an appeal to a king, but she now faces a long series of tests to prove her innocence, such as finding a tree of pure gold and a seedless grapefruit. She also must answer some riddles.

Are these merely two isolated incidents? Or are they, as a new and exhaustive report on stepmothers clearly points out, fairly indicative?

"The myth of the evil stepmother is still with us," the report concludes. "Stepmothers are still associated with the words *cruel* and *wicked*, which has made them easy targets for torture and banishment as well as severely limiting their employment, particularly in the so-called 'caring' professions such as nursing, social work, and education. The myth that stepmothers use poisons and potions has virtually barred them from the food and drug industries. In general, stepmothers are not only underpaid and underemployed but also feared and despised."

How cruel is the typical stepmother?

Not very, according to the report, which examines many cases of alleged cruelty and finds almost all of them untrue. "The media have jumped on every little misunderstanding, and have blown it up to outlandish proportions," the report finds. Recently, three stepdaughters whose relationships with their stepmothers are well known agreed to speak out and set the record straight. Because each has suffered from publicity in the past and is trying to lead as normal a life as possible under the circumstances, only first names will be used.

SNOW

The story the press told was that I was in a life-threatening situation as a child and that the primary causal factor was my stepmother's envy. I can see now that there were other factors, and that *I* didn't give *her* much reinforcement—but anyway, the story was that I escaped from her and was taken in by dwarves and she found me and poisoned me with an apple and I was dead and the prince fell in love with me and brought me back to life and we got married, et cetera, et cetera. And that is what *I* believed right up to the day I walked out on him. I felt like I owed my life to Jeff because he had begged the dwarves for my body and carried it away and so the apple was shaken loose from my throat. That's why I married him. Out of gratitude.

As I look back on it, I can see that that was a very poor basis for a relationship. I was traumatized, I had been lying in a coffin under glass for *years*, and I got up and married the first guy I laid eyes on. The big prince. My hero.

Now I can see how sick our marriage was. He was always begging me to lie still and close my eyes and hold my breath. He could only relate to me as a dead person. He couldn't accept me as a living woman with needs and desires of my own. It is terribly hard for a woman to come to terms with the fact that her husband is a necrophiliac, because, of course, when it all starts, you aren't aware of what's going on—you're dead.

In trying to come to terms with myself, I've had to come to terms with my stepmother and her envy of my beauty, which made our relationship so destructive. She was a victim of the male attitude that prizes youth over maturity when it comes to women. Men can't dominate the mature woman, so they equate youth with beauty. In fact, she *was* beautiful, but the mirror (which, of course, reflected that male attitude) presented her with a poor self-image and turned her against me.

But the press never wrote the truth about that.

Or about the dwarves. All I can say is that they should have been named Dopey, Sleepy, Slimy, Sleazy, Dirty, Disgusting, and Sexist. The fact is that I *knew* the apple was poisoned. For me, it was the only way out.

GRETEL

When Hansel and I negotiated the sale of book rights to Grimm Bros., he and I retained the right of final approval of the manuscript and agreed to split the proceeds fifty-fifty. We shook hands on it and I thought the deal was set, but then his lawyers put me under a spell, and when I woke up, they had rewritten the contract and the book too! I couldn't believe it! Not only did the new contract cut me out (under the terms, I was to get ten shiny baubles out of the first fortune the book earned and three trinkets for each additional fortune) but the book was pure fiction.

Suddenly he was portrayed as the strong and resourceful one, a regular little knight, and I came off as a weak sister. Dad was shown as a loving father who was talked into abandoning us in the forest by Gladys, our "wicked" stepmother.

Nothing could be further from the truth.

My brother was a basket case from the moment the birds ate his bread crumbs. He lay down in a heap and whimpered, and I had to slap him a couple times *hard* to make him walk. Now the little wiener makes himself out to be the hero who kept telling me, "Don't cry, Gretel." Ha! The only crying I did was from sheer exhaustion carrying him on my back.

As for Dad, he was no bleeding heart. He was very much into that whole woodcutter/peasant/yeoman scene—cockfighting, bullbaiting, going to the village on Saturday to get drunk and watch a garroting or a boiling—don't kid yourself, Gladys couldn't send us to our *rooms* without his say-so. The truth is that he was in favor of the forest idea from the word go.

What I can't understand is why they had to lie about it. Many, *many* parents left their children in the forest in those days. It was nothing unusual.

Nowadays, we tend to forget that famine can be a very difficult experience for a family. For many parents, ditching the kids was not only a solution, it was an act of faith. They believed that ravens would bring morsels of food in their beaks, or that wolves would take care of the kids, or a frog would, or that the fairies would step in. Dwarves, a hermit, a band of pilgrims, a kindly shepherd, *somebody*. And they were right.

And that is why I was never seriously worried for one single moment while we were there. Deep down, I always knew we would make it.

I don't mean to say that it wasn't a trying experience, an *emotional* experience. It was. And yet there isn't a single documented case of a child left in the forest who suffered any lasting damage. You look at those children today and you will find they are better people for having gone through it. Except for my brother, that is. The little jerk. He and my father live in luxurious manors with beautiful tapestries and banners and ballrooms, and I live above an alchemist's shop in a tiny garret they call a condo. As for Gladys, she was kicked out without so much as a property settlement. She didn't even get half of the hut. I guess she is the one who suffered most. Her and the witch.

I often think about the witch—I ask myself, Why did I give her the shove? After all, it wasn't me she was after.

I guess that, back then, I wasn't prepared to understand her type of militance. I couldn't see that she was fattening up Hansel in order to make a very radical statement. If only I had. Not that I necessarily would have joined her in making that statement, but I would have seen that from her point of view it had validity and meaning.

And I would have seen that Gladys, in proposing the forest as a viable alternative, was offering me independence at a very early age.

I wish I had been able to thank her.

CINDERELLA

A woman in my position does not find it easy to "come out of the palace," so to speak, and to provide intimate details of her personal life. I do so only because I believe it is time to put the Cinderella myth to rest once and for all—the myth that one can escape housework by marrying a prince.

The truth is that I am busier than ever. Supervising a large household staff—cooks, maids, footmen, pages, ladies-in-waiting, minstrels and troubadours, a bard or two—is just plain hard work. Often I find myself longing for the "good old days" when my stepmother made me sweep the hearth.

We see each other almost every day—she comes up here and we play tennis or I go down there for lunch—and we often reminisce and laugh about our little disagreements. She is one of my best friends. Other people treat me like royalty but she treats me like a real person. My husband won't let me touch a broom, but I go to her house and she puts me to work! I love it. I tell her, "Mother, you're the only one who yells at me. Don't ever stop." And I mean it. Anger is real. It's honest.

Honesty is a rare commodity in a palace, and that is why so many "fairy-tale" marriages end up on the rocks. You wouldn't believe the amount of fawning and flattering that goes on! Between the courtiers bowing and scraping and the suppliants and petitioners wheedling and whining, and the scheming of bishops and barons, not to mention the sorcery and witchcraft, the atmosphere is such that it's terribly hard for a man and a woman to establish a loving, trusting, sharing type of relationship.

It's true that we lived happily ever after, but believe me, we have had to work at it!

PLAINFOLKS

*A Handbook of Survival Skills, Folkways,
Practical Wisdom, and Useful Information,
Compiled from Original Sources and Reflecting
"The Way It Used to Be"*

PREFACE

When several of my twelfth-grade English students approached
me last winter with the idea of putting out a book of local
folkways and folklore, I was frankly skeptical. So many such
books have been published lately, showing how to make cane
baskets, spin wool, deliver babies, build log cabins, bake corn
pone, call hogs, pluck chickens, and so on, that I doubted that
any lore remained undiscovered. Then, too, our school is located
in a fairly new suburb. Thirty years ago, there was nothing here
but miles of swamp and the Farrell Mink Farm.

Fortunately, I gave my permission, and the result is *Plainfolks*. Except for some editing here and there, it is entirely a

student project, and it began last October during our two-week section on Tom Wolfe, when one of the boys brought a model of a 1957 Chevrolet to class. Suddenly everyone became very interested. How was the chassis lowered? Why? What was the technical term for the chrome-plated exhaust pipes extending from the engine? Soon we were discussing the fifties and sixties in terms of real people and what they had actually done. It made literature come alive.

To learn more, the students borrowed tape recorders from the Media Center and went home to interview older brothers and sisters, neighbors, and others who had firsthand knowledge of the period. For many students, this was their first real attempt at communication with the older generation. They discovered that these persons have much to teach us, if only we are willing to listen. That is the true purpose of *Plainfolks*.

BOOKCASES

Kenny Dodge lives in a three-room apartment near the university, where he has resided ever since he was a student there fourteen years ago. He is a tall, soft-spoken man, who enjoys telling stories about his work with the Fair Play for Cuba Committee, the Freedom Rides, and other historic events he remembers from his youth. While we were visiting him one evening, we noticed several handmade bookcases in the living room and asked him to tell us how he had made them.

"This is a simple bookcase," he said, pointing to the shelves behind his chair. "You pile four bricks on the floor to support a plank—two bricks at either end—then more bricks on that plank to support a second plank, and so on. The thickness of the plank sort of depends on how heavy the books are. You just have to judge for yourself. I prefer old bricks, but new ones would work, too, I suppose.

"Over here is the kind of bookcase you have to nail together. You lay it all out on the floor and make sure all the shelves are the same length. Then you nail the sides to the shelves. You have to be sure to nail each shelf at both ends—otherwise, of course, it won't hold. And be sure to put your heavier books on the lower shelves and the light ones on the upper shelves. If you do it the other way around, it could fall right down on top of you."

DAVE LA PRESTI

Way out in Apple Ridge, beyond the airport, lives Dave La Presti, with his wife, Ann, and their two children, Craig and Dale. The house is hard to find, tucked back in the woods at the end of Belle Vista Drive. The La Prestis have named their house and half acre "Casa Verde." "We enjoy the quiet out here, and everything is a lot simpler than in the city," Dave explains. "I can take the Interstate and be at work in twenty-five minutes."

Dave is an accomplished craftsman and has built most of the lamps and tables in the house. Ann makes many of her own clothes. Both boys make birdhouses, which they sell to neighbors. We had heard about Dave from the older brother of one of the girls in the class, who told us Dave could blow smoke rings better than anyone else he knew. We asked Dave to show us how, and he lit up a cigarette.

"You have to take in enough smoke to blow three or four rings," he said. "The first one generally isn't much good, but you can make adjustments for the next one and then get off a couple of real dandies. You don't inhale, of course, and you don't really *blow* the smoke. You sort of squeeze it out around your tongue with your cheeks. Like this." He blew a ring. "If you do it right, it should have a slight clockwise spin on it.

Watch." He blew another. "A good ring'll hold its shape all the way to the ceiling."

He told us he had heard of a man who used to be able to blow smoke rings out of his nose. "I never saw it, myself," he said. "I doubt that it will ever be done again."

A few minutes later, while we were saying goodbye, he blew another smoke ring for us—a beauty. "The old man can still cut it," he said, chuckling. "It can't really be taught," he added. "Either you've got it or you don't."

SNOW ART

Mary McDermott: "In the winter when I was a kid, we'd all go outside to play in the snow—*all* of us kids would do it. Nowadays, I don't know, it just seems there's less of that. But back then we'd be outside havin' fun. At least, we thought it was fun. Of course, maybe fun was different then. Fun was what you *made* it, y'know. Today, I don't know, seems like kids have to have their fun made *for* 'em. Anyway, we useta make angels in the snow. We'd lay down and slide our arms up 'n' down to make the wings and our legs back 'n' forth to make the robe. That was fun. And then on the school bus, y'know, the windows would be all frosted up, and we'd stick our fists on'm to make little footprints. Or blow on'm and make holes in the frost. You don't see so many angels or footprints anymore. . . . Of course, they do still build snowmen, but they don't work so hard at 'em. We useta pour water on ours, and it'd freeze and they'd keep till spring. That was something, I'll tell you. I'm thirty-two now, and I remember us doing all that. It was a custom, I guess—all of us kids would do it. Nowadays, I don't know."

DON WOJCAK

Many model-railroad sets are sold today, but most are discarded after a few years, and few track owners ever develop a complex, totally integrated layout with a realistic landscape. We looked at dozens of small layouts, most of them kept on Ping-Pong tables in basements, before we found Don Wojcak, a postal supervisor who's been developing his layout since World War II. His spread now occupies the entire third floor of the large colonial home where Don grew up and where he now lives with his wife and parents.

The Wojcak layout, which is $^{17}/_{64}$-inch scale, includes four towns (named after his aunts) of approximately fifty homes apiece; a hydroelectric plant on a recirculating river, both built to scale; and ten trains—two passenger, eight freight—that run on regular schedules. There are four additional freight trains that operate during grain (actually, a very fine brown sand) harvest, and a ski train.

"Most builders lose interest eventually, because they don't work on the layout every day," Don told us. "You have to put in a regular shift, otherwise it gets dull. But when you keep at it, keep adding to it—new ideas, new developments—you keep seeing new things to do. For example, I'm getting more and more interested in community planning and thinking in terms of twenty, thirty years from now—more high-density housing in revitalized inner-city neighborhoods, with industrial nodes shielded by greenways. Of course, trains are the main thing, but lately we've been doing a lot of work on recreational facilities. We put in a lake and a campground, two new parks, and a Teen Rec."

One problem for model-railroad builders has always been grass. Don started out with green felt, then experimented with artificial grass carpeting, and then settled on velvet. However, now he is gradually switching over to an artificial surface material called MiniTurf. It has a grasslike texture and it tends to turn brown during summer months.

Another problem is the sky. For years, Don made do with blue ceiling-and-wall paint and a central overhead spotlight.

But since he went to work on the day shift at the post office he has painted the walls and ceiling black, removed the spotlight, and installed a scale-model lighting system on the layout. The Milky Way is made entirely of sequins, but it looks like stars.

ARLEN L. POWELL

None of the *Plainfolks* staff has gotten in a fight since grade school, and so we were immediately interested when we had a staff party at the Big Boy Drive-in one night and a short-haired, heavyset man came over to the car and offered to shove our faces in. His name was Arlen L. Powell, he told us, and he didn't care for the way in which we were looking at him. After we apologized for the misunderstanding, however, he became friendlier and agreed to answer our questions if we didn't get smart with him, which we promised not to.

Arlen said he believes in keeping his hands to himself but if people try to walk all over him they should watch out. He said that everyone who fights him knows they are in a fight. They don't come around his parking space again. In fact, Arlen controls four spaces at the Big Boy, which are the four in back of the building, by the men's lavatory. Arlen keeps these spaces for himself and his friends, who have patronized the Big Boy since 1958, when it was built. That evening, we observed him defend the area several times. Generally speaking, his methods of defense are as follows:

1. *Distant early warning:* Anyone who approaches the area receives a warning at a distance; it is designed to make him think twice before coming closer—e.g., "Butt out, pinhead."

2. *Psychological delay:* Insistent trespassers are allowed to come well within the crucial boundaries before Arlen makes his move.

3. *Sudden attack:* Arlen moves fast.

4. *Sustained momentum:* Arlen hits high (a hard, bumping shove) and keeps going until he has the trespasser backed against the wall or a car.

5. *Second warning and release:* This warning was inaudible, since it was hissed. Arlen then released the trespasser by pushing him hard in the direction of the area from which he had come.

The trespassers left Arlen's area after their release. Arlen permitted them to yell face-saving remarks ("You're gonna regret this!" "I'll be back later!") over the shoulder without running after them and pounding them. He only does that, he told us, if they are not maintaining steady progress in the opposite (or *away*) direction as they yell.

ART AND BUD

Arlen L. Powell recommended two men as sources of information about car customizing, and we met them one evening in a bar on Lake Street. Both told us that the subject was too vast to cover in one evening. One said it was something you had to grow up with. Nevertheless, they agreed to talk about it in general terms. Neither of them drives a customized car today. It requires complete dedication, they said, and besides, they are married and have kids, and "as you get older your interests change," as one of them put it. Both agreed that top-quality customizing is pretty much a thing of the past.

Bud: "I see kids ambling up and down Lake in their little transbucket Mustangs, it's totally ridiculous to me. I am unable to understand this. I remember when a guy'd work his butt off to make something worth being seen in—chopped, channeled, bored, and stroked. Dual quads, scavenger pipes, Baby Moons, big Offy manifold, flames painted on the hood, dingleberries in the window, carpet on the floor, fur around the mirror—I mean, we did a *number* on it. There was pride at one time.

Now, as I say, it's ludicrous. These guys have nothing and they don't even know it. They don't care."

Art: "There was something under the hood in those days—you knew, because you'd *put* it there—and if you didn't have it, you kept off the street or got blown out of the water in a hurry. I had a full-house Ford—four on the floor, geared down deep. When you stuck your foot in it, she'd lay rubber into next week. Other day, I'm coming home from work in my wife's car—my *wife's* car, this *sled*—and a kid pulls up at the stoplight in a *Rambler* and guns it. One of the most pitiful sounds I ever heard. I am ready to *weep*. Light turns green, I ooze away in the slushbox, and this kid can't locate first gear. It makes you sick to see it."

Us: "Why don't they make them like you used to?"

Bud: "They're lazy! They walk onto a lot and say, 'Gimme that one,' and that's it. They drive it until it rusts out, and trade it in. When we bought a car, that was only the beginning. We'd work three months just to make it fit to be seen. On Lake Street, that is. Of course, you could drive anything down Portland or out Fiftieth. But we're talking about *Lake* Street."

Art: "It's a matter of pride. Back then, I'd take the Ford around town, wind it out, listen to the pipes pop. It made me feel good. Like I *had* something. I'd sit down low in her and drive around all night—down Lake to the drive-in, turn around, back up Lake to Excelsior Boulevard, turn around, back down Lake—do that for hours. Two tanks of gas in one night. Nowadays, everybody's in a hurry. They just want to get there. They don't care, don't care what anybody thinks, don't care how they look—just get there. Rush, rush, rush. In our day, we took it easy. Up and back. Up and back. It was beautiful."

THE PEOPLE'S SHOPPER

Shop the Co-op Way and Save!
These Fine Peoples Are Happy to Serve You

THE WHOLE WHEAT FOOD CO-OP

The WWFC Coordinating Council has approved the following statement for publication. The Council voted on the statement line by line, and where the vote was not unanimous the minority opinion appears in brackets.

WHOLE WHEAT FLOUR Ground on Our Own Millstone 12¢ lb. [8¢]

ORANGES 6¢ ea.

MILK 39¢ ¹/₂ gal. 82¢ gal. [*What's the markup for—the pleasure of your company?* 78¢]

CARROTS 15¢ lb. [*The carrots are not too crisp because the big honchos in this so-called organization don't know how to call an electrician to fix the cooler, which has not worked for six weeks now. In fact, it's like a steam pit in there. If the "coordinators" would come around once in a while they might find out about these things. The oranges are shriveled up, also the lettuce, and the carrots are like rubber. Organic or not, I wouldn't feed it to apes. Diane.*]

HOME-MADE YOGHURT Delicious 75¢ qt. [*Anyone who can in good conscience sell this stuff for 75¢ should be forced to eat it.*]

ACORN SQUASH 30¢ ea. [*I will not accept more than 21¢ per squash and I am giving away the bread and milk free until this group shows a little more sensitivity to the women, who do about two-thirds of the work. That's no lie, either.*

I am at the store 1–4 P.M. Mondays and 5–8 Thursdays— the tall woman with reddish hair and glasses. See me for bargains. Marcia.]

SHARP CHEDDAR 80¢ lb. [*Stuff it in your ear, hippie ripoff artist! We're busting out of this pukehole!*]

SUPPORT [*The Boycott of*] YOUR NEIGHBORHOOD CO-OP!

PEOPLE'S CANDY COLLECTIVE

Last August, five of us pulled out of the Whole Wheat Co-op to form the Collective. Hopefully this article will try to explain what we're doing and where we go from here.

At Whole Wheat we were making sesame-seed cakes and oat balls. We enjoyed our work, but we wanted to branch out into wholesome chocolates and nut bars. This proved to be traumatic for the Co-op hierarchy, which was into macrobiotic and organic gardening, the whole elitist grocery bag. They took the position that candy is bad for the people, it ruins their teeth, spoils their appetite, etc. Finally, we split. Our purpose was to set up a candy store where the decision-making would be shared by the whole community and everyone could contribute his ideas.

First, we visited the existing candy store in the neighborhood, Yaklich's. We assured Mr. Yaklich and his son Baron that our intention was to cooperate, not compete, and we agreed not to sell cigarettes, cigars, newspapers, magazines, or adult books, which they are very much into. They are also into point spreads, and we agreed not to do that, either.

Second, we tried to get some Indian, black, and Chicano representation (of which there was none) in the Collective, but that was a problem, since there was none in the neighborhood, either, and attendance at our meetings would've meant a long ride on the bus for them.

Finally, we began soliciting community input. We began at the nearby grade school, where we met a lot of people who, though unfamiliar with the theory of running a collective, were very helpful and gave us a lot of new ideas. They suggested such things as licorice whips, nougat bars, sourballs, jawbreakers, bubble gum, soda pop, Popsicles, cupcakes, and Twinkies.

These are yet to be discussed, but it appears we have several alternatives: to go back to Whole Wheat, to help the grade-school community set up its own candy collective, or to serve them and their needs in order to create a broader base of support within which we can seek to familiarize them with where we are at. We invite anyone concerned to stop by the store (upstairs from the Universal Joint).

St. Paul's Episcopal
Drop-in Hair Center

If you've decided to get a haircut, that's your decision, but why go to a straight barber and pay $3.50 for a lot of bad jokes? Come to St. Paul's Hair Center (in the rectory basement) where Rev. Ray and Rev. Don are waiting to see you. The price is right on and the rap is easy. Ray and Don are trained barbers, but more than that they know how hard this move can be and offer warm supportive pre- and post-trim counseling. They're people-oriented, not hair-oriented, and if you just want to come in and *talk* about haircuts, well, that's cool, too.

PEOPLE'S MEATS

Most of us accept strict vegetarianism as the best way, but many find it difficult to change their eating habits. People's Meats is an interim solution. All of our meat comes from animals who were unable to care for themselves any longer. Hoping to phase out the operation, we do not advertise hours, prices, or location. We do not deliver.

PEOPLE'S USED FURNITURE

One sign of what's going on in our society is the trend toward larger and harder beds. Queen-size, wider, firmer—beds that resemble a flat plain and the sleepers ships passing in the night, not knowing one another at all. We reject that kind of sleep with our Warm Valley Bed. It is narrow and soft and shaped like a trough, gently urging its occupants toward the middle. No matter how hard you fight it (and we all do), the Warm Valley Bed brings the two of you together into warm mutually reinforcing physical contact. The bed of commitment. Specify depth.

THE UNIVERSAL JOINT GARAGE & BODY SHOP

The way it is at the U.J. is like the five of us, Sully, Bill, Butch, Duke, and Bud, we're totally together because we stay high together and when you come in with your car, say the car is really bummed out and won't even start, before we even *touch* that car we're going to sit down with you and get you up there together with us.

Now, a lot of folks can't dig that. They say, "Here's my car. When can you fix it?" or some other kind of linear crap. Well, we just got to talk that person loose. Because we are not in that *fix* matrix at all. We say, "We're not there yet. We're *here*." Or we say, "You on a wrench trip? O.K., here's a wrench!" But that's not where he's at or the car either, and on a simple planetary level they both know it. The car and him are one circuit, one continuum, and the ignition switch is right there in his head. Like we say, "The key is *not* the key! Tools are *not* the tools!"

So what we do is get very loose and very easy and very high. The afternoon goes by and the whole shop is like suspended up there in its own holding pattern, we're all sitting around listening to the leak in the air hose and *digging* it, and slowly that person gets to copping to that car through us. It's tremendous, a stone—you feel the energy really flowing. So we're all sitting there revving on *that* and then the car starts to get off on it and pretty soon that *car* gets going. Sometimes it starts by itself, other times we got to do some laying on of hands, but it's *going.* Wide open, you can feel it vibrating. So all that comes right back to *us.* Like the car is going *rmmm-rmmm-rmmm* and *we're* going *rmmm-rmmm-rmmm*, and the next thing you know that person gets in the car and he just like takes *off!* Which was his Karma all this time—to *go.* Like he was in this place, now he's in another place, pretty soon he'll be somewhere else, and so on, but you know, it's all one road.

THE PHANTOM STOMACH
ALTERNATIVE CAFÉ

The Stomach originated as a study group within the Whole Wheat Co-op, for people interested in vegetables as a tool in therapy. We were somewhat divided between eggplant and kohlrabi, but we got along pretty well. All of us felt that eating vegetables helped us free ourselves from authoritarian life-systems and become more self-sufficient and honest with ourselves and more whole. Wholeness was the key. But as we pushed it farther we came to feel that vegetables were merely raising us to a higher ego-level that was rather empty and intellectual. We felt whole but we didn't feel full. It was then that we discovered "the other stomach."

The group was on a five-day fast in order to get beyond food and onto a different thought plane where we could meditate with our stomachs and find out what they wanted. One night we went up to the roof of an apartment building to cool off, and as we lay there we saw a great membrane descending from the sky. The membrane shone with a pale moist light. As it came near, we saw hamburgers in it, a thousand of them, and pizzas—pepperoni, sausage, anchovy-and-sausage, mushroom —along with French fries, Cokes, onion rings, Big Macs, Pronto Pups, chow mein, Reubens, malts, frosted doughnuts, buttered popcorn—everything right there within reach. We heard tremendous bursts of thunder from the membrane, and then a voice said, "Eat!"

We said, "But we can't. We're fasting, and besides it's not our kind of food."

And it said again, louder, "Eat!"

So we did—the stuff looked good—and to our surprise, it *was* good. It was hot and tasty and crisp, and the more we ate the more there was of it. We kept saying, "It *is* our thing, it *is* our thing!" Because we'd never felt that way before. A spreading circle of warmth from the stomach to all parts of the body. A great calorie rush.

The next night, we'd invited all of our friends. Hundreds of people joined in the feast. There was enough for everyone and we became aware of a very profound physical sensation that we never got from vegies. Now we know: Around the little vegetable stomach there is a second and much greater stomach, which eggplant cannot satisfy. This second stomach is the whole body. As the voice said to us the second night, "You are not *what* you eat. You *are* eating." You only realize that if you eat the right food.

We're trying to carry out this philosophy in our café. We sell burgers that make people listen to themselves and understand themselves, and we got a machine that turns out a single continuous French fry. The endless potato. When there are no customers in the place, we like to open the front door and let the French fry go out into the community to make contact with people. Some of them, like us, have eaten their way back to the beginning.

YOUR WEDDING AND YOU

A Few Thoughts on Making It More Personally Rewarding, Shared by Reverend Bob Osman

Courtesy of THE HUNDRED FLOWERS BRIDAL SHOP
Designers—Consultants—Caterers
"We Care"

To Howie, Chris, Lani, Kim, Steve, Greg, Sandi, Carol, Jim, Jaki,
and all the young people who taught me to love them

> In the gentle happy mornin'
> Of the country love we've known,
> Let's build a life together
> And make ourselves at home.
> —Jack Aspen*

In the past decade, a very rapidly increased change in our views of marriage as an institution and the wedding ceremony as an expression of two persons' feelings about marriage and about themselves and each other, their place in the community and society, and their relationship to the planet itself (and, of course, God) has undoubtedly taken place. Perhaps this change is summed up fairly well by two young people whom I'll call *Pat* and *Mike*.

"People like us reject the stereotypes, the role-playing, that seem to be so much a part of other people's relationships," they confided to me one day during premarital counseling. "We are individuals with an infinite capacity for loving, sharing, knowing, caring, growing, and expanding. We want our wedding to express that unique personalness, that *beingness*, that each of us, and only us, can bring to marriage. Do you know what we mean?"

More and more, most of us do—especially those in the eighteen-to-thirty-five age group in which most first marriages take place. Oftentimes writing their own ceremonies and creating their own symbols, language, music, feelings, this generation of young couples is seeking new modes, new marriage styles, to express what one minister called "the naturally religious, the realistically mystical, the practically impossible."

Heavy, right?

Not necessarily. In fact, the emphasis is definitely *away* from heaviness and *toward* lightness and informality. Comfortable. Feeling good. Being yourself. Being okay.

That is what the "New Wedding" is all about.

What is the "New Wedding"?

O.K., let's get down to specifics.

First of all, the New Wedding is less likely to occur in a formal place of worship or government but, rather, in an environment where the couple feels comfortable—a natural hillside or valley, a favorite restaurant, a nearby park or playground, or the home of a close friend.

Second, it is less likely to involve formal Judeo-Christian-establishment language but, rather, words that the couple would want to say to each other even if they weren't getting married.

Third, it is more likely to make each person attending the ceremony feel like a participant in something that is very interesting indeed.

Of course, many couples still elect a more traditional ceremony: the white tunics and daisy crowns, the lighting of matches by the congregation, the beautiful Peter, Paul, and Mary songs, and such a ceremony can be deeply meaningful in its own way. Certainly no couple should reject it just to be "different." An Alternative Wedding should be chosen only after careful and sincere discussion of the couple's own values, dreams, and attitudes at this most important moment in their life.

What is an "Alternative Wedding"?

That's a good question. I'd say, "It depends pretty much on the individual," so let's look at some individual cases.

Sam and *Judy*, for example. They chose to emphasize their mutual commitment to air and water quality, exchanging vows while chained to each other and to the plant gate of a major industrial polluter.

Lyle and *Marcia*, recognizing their dependence on each other, were joined in matrimony in a crowd of total strangers and had but $3.85 and a couple of tokens between them.

Al and *Tammy*, on the other hand, sharing a commitment to challenge and excitement, were married in 6.12 seconds in *Al's* Supercharged Funny Car, with a minister on her lap and four bridesmaids on the floor (a new track record).

Bud and *Karen* chose a simple ceremony in their own apartment, with *Karen* fixing pizza in the kitchen, *Bud* asleep on the sofa, and their *two children* watching television in the bedroom.

Charles and *Frank*, however, selected the Early Traditional style, complete with morning coats, Wagner and Mendelssohn, and crustless sandwiches.

Others have been married in canoes or small powerboats, under bridges, in tunnels, beside creeks, on towers, over the telephone (with the groom calling from a distant tavern), and on ski tows, islands, mountain peaks, peninsulas, rooftops, and rocks. A New, or Alternative, Wedding means freedom to be married in exactly the way you always wanted to be.

What is an "Alternative, or New, Wedding"?

Very well, let's look at three basic elements of the marriage ceremony in terms of personal experience today: readings, or literature; ceremony itself, or drama; and singing, or music. All are forms of *celebration*, from the Latin word *celebratio*, meaning "to get along famously, or quickly."

MUSIC: The music of Scott Joplin, Bob Dylan, Barbra Streisand, the Carpenters, the Grateful Dead, "Sesame Street," Pepsi-Cola, and the Fifties is often chosen, though many couples are now creating their own music. *Henry* and *Phyllis* were members of the Beloveds, a bliss-rock band, and decided to hold their wedding in a large auditorium, with a sellout crowd sharing the joy and excitement of a Beloveds concert. Although the band had never played outside of small coffeehouses and was little known on the music scene, with the help and concern of a supportive promoter the concert was arranged, with ticket prices scaled upward accordingly. "It was a wonderful wedding, and we all got off on it, especially the aspect of total sharing," remarked *Phyllis* afterward. "And there would've been even more to share, except the promoter took 60 percent off the top, and expenses wiped out the rest. Which goes to show the importance of having a good wedding contract." Alternatively, you may want to invite guests to bring their own instruments or a favorite record.

CEREMONY: It is customary for the bride and groom to write their own ceremony, reflecting their own tastes suitable to the occasion. *Vern* and *LaVerne* wanted their wedding to be a "rite of passage" from the empty, structured urban life they had known to a new rural life based on community and trusting and showing concern for tradition and love of the land, and they set out to do exactly that. Leaving the midwestern city in which they had long lived, the couple drove south looking for a community that was just right. A few hours later, they came across a small white frame church in the country. Its oak-shaded yard was crowded with aged parishioners eating fried-chicken lunches and displaying native crafts and abilities. The minister, a kindly old man in a black frock coat and starched shirt, greeted them warmly, and when *Vern* and *LaVerne* indicated their intentions he let out a joyous yell and slapped his thigh. "Bust my buttons! Caroline, fetch my collar!" he whooped and shouted. In no time, the entire congregation was seated in the church and singing old-time shape-note hymns, fanning vigorously, and crying "Amen!" at every opportunity.

Minister: "Well, Lord, You sure gave us one heck of a hard winter and I reckon some of us wondered if there'd be no end to it, but, dang it, this troubled ol' earth just keeps a-rotatin' and here we are at plantin' time agin and the trees are puttin' out their blossoms and the ol' bull is lookin' across the fence at the heifers and it sorta speaks to us of what they call *renewal* and *rededication*, don't it?

"And that's why we're here today, ain't it, Lord, 'cause these-here kids want ter sorta carry on them *natural processes* and kinder do their part to *create life* and be what Y'might call *at one* with You and each other and the trees and the birds and this great big ball of humanity we got down here and what we might call the *life force*—anyhow, that's the way I see it.

"Well, Lord, they're a-waitin' for me, and Caroline here is clearin' her throat somethin' fierce, so I guess I said enough, but—well, You take real good care of 'em now, Y'hear? Goodbye, God. Be talkin' to Y'later."

Vern and *LaVerne* also wrote their own vows. *Rod* and *Mary Elizabeth*, on the other hand, employed the regular vows of their church but added two pages of dialogue from *Love Knows No Night*—a scene in which *Curly* and *Jo-Jo*, pi ed by the mud slide, promise to love each other forever if they are rescued soon. Or a couple might wish to speak extemporaneously.

LITERATURE: Readings from Walt Whitman, Thoreau, Dylan Thomas, E. E. Cummings, Frost, the Song of Solomon, and Carl Rogers are popular at weddings today, and, properly chosen, can be every bit as personal and creative as your own poems, essays, songs, or articles. The key, of course, is to make them your own, expressing your own feelings and desires.

Sometimes, selections may be incorporated into the ceremony itself. (Some states have recognized Marlowe's "Come live with me and be my love" as a legally binding contract, but be sure to check with local authorities about this, to avoid misunderstandings later.) Or you might want to write your own dialogue and incorporate *that* into the ceremony, as a young couple did not long ago who asked that their names not be used:

Man: And shall we then be husband and wife, and love and trust each other in the spirit of mutual adventure and joy, giving nurture and sustenance the one to the other and yet also preserving the independence and solitude of each, W——?

Woman: I—I—don't know what to say . . . just that I'm . . .

Man: I'm here. Cleave to me.

Woman: . . . so happy. Happy and mixed up and—I don't know. It's like—

Man: Like we were two but now we are two in one?

Woman: Like what Carl Rogers once wrote. "When I love you, I am loving myself, for you are me."

Man: "When you love me, you are loving yourself, for I am you."

Both: "When we love ourselves, we are loving the world, for we are it."

Woman: P——, read that short poem you wrote for us recently.

Man: Oh, I don't know—it's sort of personal.

Woman: Please.

Man: Well, all right:

> maybe it will always be that sunday
>   when
> we sang to the little bouncing ball
>   dribbled
> down the dewy grass-green fair-
>   ways of our
> consciousness landing in hard woods
>   of where
> and when   so let us always
> and not just the day before tomor-
>   row slice
> together the loaf of our caring and
>   hook
> the fish of our first flowing self no
> kidding swinging love's clubs be-
>   tween
> the hazards of water the traps of
>   sand
> in the baggy morning crazy happy
>   yelling "For! For!"

Woman: P——!

Man: W——!

Or you might enclose your poem in the wedding invitation or have it printed on napkins. *Stan* and *Debbie*, although they were not poets, nonetheless wanted their wedding to be a "marriage of minds" and a time of sharing with family and friends, and sent out the invitations three months before, including a short reading list:

> *Bhagavad Gita*
> *Couples*, Updike
> *Crime and Punishment*, Dostoevski
> *The Golden Bough*, Frazer
> *The Great Gatsby*, Fitzgerald
> *How to Be Your Own Best Friend*, Newman and
>   Berkowitz
> *On Aggression*, Lorenz
> *The Portable Nietzsche*, Nietzsche
> *The Republic*, Plato
> *Them*, Oates
> *We*, Lindbergh

In the church, the couple entered together from the rear and sat in front facing the guests. The attendants passed up and down the aisles distributing notebooks and pencils. The minister introduced *Stan* and *Debbie*, who took turns addressing the audience from a small lectern. *Debbie* spoke on "Views of Home in Post-Marriage Culture." *Stan* spoke on "The Goddess and the Mom: Woman as Totemic Figure and Family Technician in Contemporary Mythology." After a brief discussion and a multiple-choice quiz, the service was over. (To conserve time, *Stan* and *Debbie* had been married three weeks before at their apartment.)

Or you can simply speak to each guest briefly during the reception, to make sure the main points of your wedding are clearly understood. And if you have already selected your married life-style you may wish to discuss that, too. (See my "Choosing a Life-style" or call me and make an appointment.)

SHY RIGHTS:
WHY NOT PRETTY SOON?

Recently I read about a group of fat people who had organized to fight discrimination against themselves. They said that society oppresses the overweight by being thinner than them and that the term "overweight" itself is oppressive because it implies a "right" weight that the fatso has failed to make. Only weightists use such terms, they said; they demanded to be called "total" people and to be thought of in terms of wholeness; and they referred to thin people as being "not all there."

Don't get me wrong. This is fine with me. If, to quote the article if I may, "Fat Leaders Demand Expanded Rights Act, Claim Broad Base of Support," I have no objections to it whatsoever. I feel that it is their right to speak up and I admire them for doing so, though of course this is only my own opinion. I could be wrong.

Nevertheless, after reading the article, I wrote a letter to

President Jimmy Carter demanding that his administration take action to end discrimination against shy persons sometime in the very near future. I pointed out three target areas—laws, schools, and attitudes—where shy rights maybe could be safeguarded. I tried not to be pushy but I laid it on the line. "Mr. President," I concluded, "you'll probably kill me for saying this but compared to what you've done for other groups, we shys have settled for 'peanuts.' As you may know, we are not ones to make threats, but it is clear to me that if we don't get some action on this, it could be a darned quiet summer. It is up to you, Mr. President. Whatever you decide will be okay by me. Yours very cordially."

I never got around to mailing the letter, but evidently word got around in the shy community that I had written it, and I've noticed that most shy persons are not speaking to me these days. I guess they think the letter went too far. Probably they feel that making demands is a betrayal of the shy movement (or "gesture," as many shys call it) and an insult to shy pride and that it risks the loss of some of the gains we have already made, such as social security and library cards.

Perhaps they are right. I don't claim to have all the answers. I just feel that we ought to begin, at least, to think about some demands that we *might* make if, for example, we *had* to someday. That's all. I'm not saying we should make fools of ourselves, for heaven's sake!

Shut Up (A Slogan)

Sometimes I feel that maybe we shy persons have borne our terrible burden for far too long now. Labeled by society as "wimps," "dorks," "creeps," and "sissies," stereotyped as Milquetoasts and Walter Mittys, and tagged as potential psychopaths ("He kept pretty much to himself," every psychopath's landlady is quoted as saying after the arrest, and for weeks thereafter every shy person is treated like a leper), we shys are desperately misunderstood on every hand. Because we don't "talk out" our feelings, it is assumed that we haven't any. It is assumed that we never exclaim, retort, or cry out, though naturally we do on occasions when it seems called for.

Would anyone dare to say to a woman or a Third World person, "Oh, don't be a woman! Oh, don't be so Third!"? And yet people make bold with us whenever they please and put an arm around us and tell us not to be shy.

Hundreds of thousands of our shy brothers and sisters (and "cousins twice-removed," as militant shys refer to each other) are victimized every year by self-help programs that promise to "cure" shyness through hand-buzzer treatments, shout training, spicy diets, silence-aversion therapy, and every other gimmick in the book. Many of them claim to have "overcome" their shyness, but the sad fact is that they are afraid to say otherwise.

To us in the shy movement, however, shyness is not a disability or disease to be "overcome." It is simply the way we are. And in our own quiet way, we are secretly proud of it. It isn't something we shout about at public rallies and marches. It is Shy Pride. And while we don't have a Shy Pride Week, we do have many private moments when we keep our thoughts to ourselves, such as "Shy is nice," "Walk short," "Be proud—shut up," and "Shy is beautiful, for the most part." These are some that I thought up myself. Perhaps other shy persons have some of their own, I don't know.

A "Number One" Disgrace

Discrimination against the shy is our country's number one disgrace in my own personal opinion. Millions of men and women are denied equal employment, educational and recreational opportunities, and rewarding personal relationships simply because of their shyness. These injustices are nearly impossible to identify, not only because the shy person will not speak up when discriminated against, but also because the shy person almost always *anticipates* being denied these rights and doesn't ask for them in the first place. (In fact, most shys will politely decline a right when it is offered to them.)

Most shy lawyers agree that shys can never obtain justice under our current adversary system of law. The Sixth Amendment, for example, which gives the accused the right to confront his accusers, is anti-shy on the face of it. It effectively denies shy persons the right to accuse anyone of anything.

One solution might be to shift the burden of proof to the defendant in case the plaintiff chooses to remain silent. Or we could create a special second-class citizenship that would take away some rights, such as free speech, bearing arms, and running for public office, in exchange for some other rights that we need more. In any case, we need some sort of fairly totally new concept of law if we shys are ever going to enjoy equality, if indeed that is the sort of thing we could ever enjoy.

A MILLION-DOLLAR RIPOFF

Every year, shy persons lose millions of dollars in the form of overcharges that aren't questioned, shoddy products never returned to stores, refunds never asked for, and bad food in restaurants that we eat anyway, not to mention all the money we lose and are too shy to claim when somebody else finds it.

A few months ago, a shy friend of mine whom I will call Duke Hand (not his real name) stood at a supermarket checkout counter and watched the cashier ring up thirty fifteen-cent Peanut Dream candy bars and a $3.75 copy of *Playhouse* for $18.25.

He gave her a twenty-dollar bill and thanked her for his change, but as he reached for his purchases, she said, "Hold on. There's something wrong here."

"No, really, it's O.K.," he said.

"Let me see that cash register slip," she said.

"No, really, thanks anyway," he whispered. Out of the corner of his eye, he could see that he had attracted attention. Other shoppers in the vicinity had sensed that something was up, perhaps an attempted price-tag switch or insufficient identification, and were looking his way. "It's not for me," he pleaded. "I'm only buying this for a friend."

Nevertheless, he had to stand there in mute agony while she counted all of the Peanut Dreams and refigured the total and the correct change. (In fairness to her, it should be pointed out that Duke, while eventually passing on each copy of *Playhouse* to a friend, first reads it himself.)

Perhaps one solution might be for clerks and other business personnel to try to be a little bit more careful about this sort of thing in the first place. O.K.?

How About Shy History?

To many of us shys, myself included, the worst tragedy is the oppression of shy children in the schools, and while we don't presume to tell educators how to do their work, work that they have been specially trained to do, we do feel that schools must begin immediately to develop programs of shy history, or at the very least to give it a little consideration.

History books are blatantly prejudiced against shyness and shy personhood. They devote chapter after chapter to the accomplishments of famous persons and quote them at great length, and say nothing at all, or very little, about countless others who had very little to say, who never sought fame, and whose names are lost to history.

Where in the history books do we find mention of The Lady in Black, Kilroy, The Unknown Soldier, The Forgotten Man, The Little Guy, not to mention America's many noted recluses?

Where, for example, can we find a single paragraph on America's hundreds of scale models, those brave men of average height whose job it was to pose beside immense objects such as pyramids and dynamos so as to indicate scale in drawings and photographs? The only credit that scale models ever received was a line in the caption—"For an idea of its size, note man (arrow, at left)." And yet, without them, such inventions as the dirigible, the steam shovel, and the swing-span bridge would have looked like mere toys, and natural wonders such as Old Faithful, the Grand Canyon, and the giant sequoia would have been dismissed as hoaxes. It was truly a thankless job.

SHYS ON "STRIKE"

The scale models themselves never wanted any thanks. All they wanted was a rope or device of some type to keep them from falling off tall structures, plus a tent to rest in between drawings, and in 1906, after one model was carried away by a tidal wave that he had been hired to pose in front of, they formed a union and went on strike.

Briefly, the scale models were joined by a contingent of shy artists' models who had posed for what they thought was to be a small monument showing the Battle of Bull Run only to discover that it was actually a large bas-relief entitled "The Bathers" and who sat down on the job, bringing the work to a halt. While the artists' models quickly won a new contract and went back to work (on a non-representational basis), the scale models' strike was never settled.

True to their nature, the scale models did not picket the work sites or negotiate with their employers. They simply stood quietly a short distance away and, when asked about their demands, pointed to the next man. A year later, when the union attempted to take a vote on the old contract, it found that most of the scale models had moved away and left no forwarding addresses.

It was the last attempt by shy persons to organize themselves anywhere in the country.

Now Is the Time, We Think

Now is probably as good a time as any for this country to face up to its shameful treatment of the shy and to do something, almost anything, about it. On the other hand, maybe it would be better to wait for a while and see what happens. All I know is that it isn't easy trying to write a manifesto for a bunch of people who dare not speak their names. And that the shy movement is being inverted by a tiny handful of shy militants who do not speak for the majority of shy persons, nor even very often for themselves. This secret cadre, whose members are not known even to each other, advocate doing "less than nothing." They believe in tokenism, and the smaller the token the better. They seek only to promote more self-consciousness: that ultimate shyness that shy mystics call "the fear of fear itself." What is even more terrifying is the ultimate goal of this radical wing: They believe that they shall inherit the earth, and they will not stop until they do. Believe me, we moderates have our faces to the wall.

Perhaps you are saying, "What can *I* do? I share your concern at the plight of the shy and wholeheartedly endorse your two- (or three-) point program for shy equality. I pledge myself to work vigorously for its adoption. My check for ($10 $25 $50

$100 $———) is enclosed. In addition, I agree to (circulate petitions, hold fund-raising party in my home, write to congressman and senator, serve on local committee, write letters to newspapers, hand out literature door-to-door during National Friends of the Shy Drive)."

Just remember: You said it, not me.

THE LOWLIEST BUSH
A PURPLE SAGE WOULD BE

Every work of nature has a voice, poets tell us, if only we will sit quietly and listen with the "inner ear of patience and delight." The man who waits patiently for nature to speak to him will be well rewarded, they say; only he can enter into the life of silent beings and absorb their wisdom. Traditionally, American poets have listened to some things—stars, oceans, the moon, birch trees, the thrush—and ignored the rest. But some poets, such as the celebrated Arthur Newell, have followed Yin Ch'ang's admonition, "Do not / Lock the bird in the cage! / Follow it as it flies / On quick wings," and are approaching nature with an open mind.

In the Old Poetry, for example, a tree symbolized life and a bare tree meant death. But is this what the tree intended, or merely what the poet read into it? Arthur Newell may listen to a tree, an ordinary spruce, for a month and then suddenly discover that it is his mother looking out at the frozen snow of North Dakota as if her old heart would break. Or he may listen to a mandrill at the zoo and hear him say, "Forgive me for leaving Lincoln, Nebraska. / I weep for your misery. / I am no good at football."

I visited Arthur Newell this winter on his farm near Winifred, North Dakota, soon after *Cold Light of Day* (Anteater Press, $2.50) was published. He picked me up at the bus depot and we drove past the familiar "woods pleading for love" and the Little Plum River with its "mad fear of bridges."

"This is beautiful," I said, looking out at the wintry landscape.

"You impose your own concept of beauty on it," he said quietly, "because you have no wish to see what is really there underneath the surface."

I assured him that I *did* wish to see this but that I was tired from my long trip.

"At Lake Winifred / Under the clear ice, fish sing / And are truly happy," he said.

I asked him to show me the lake the next morning.

We set out at dawn across the desolate fields. They seemed desolate to me, at any rate. Soon we came to the lake, which was covered with ice and snow. As we sat on the frozen shore, we heard music that seemed to come up out of the ground. It was the deep baritone voices of walleyes under the ice singing "Her Bright Smile Haunts Me Still," "Molly Bawn," "O Haste, Crimson Morn," and other favorites. A passing female rabbit heard them, too, for she sat down near us and said, "These lovely fish / They are of the tribe of Sacajawea, / Singing in the bus depot in San Diego."

"Accountants and bank presidents skate on the ice on envelopes / Trying to forget the French Revolution," replied Arthur.

"But in the cold light / The fish study the colors of the sun," the rabbit said.

She and Arthur agreed to collaborate on a poem based on what she had heard from bears.

It isn't easy for us to observe the underlying reality of things—to know, for example, that chestnut trees are not mighty but rather shy and often superstitious about thunderstorms, that owls know very little that is worthwhile (less than most geese), or that the dish did not particularly care for the spoon, but was desperate. One must observe ". . . the silent ones / Who take short breaths" carefully if one is to learn these secrets. Stones and trees speak slowly and may take a week to get out a single sentence, and there are few men, unfortunately, with the patience to wait for an oak to finish a thought.

I know another poet who threw a rock at a squirrel who had spoken to him of "the dull light of cities / Where buses swerve and mutter like blind muskrats." The poet chased the squirrel into a pile of leaves and tried to brain him with an umbrella. "I can't walk to the corner for a loaf of bread," the poet said, "without having a dozen birds light on my shoulder and let me in on their thoughts about materialism. Or else it's some old elm on the boulevard who thinks he's my uncle, restless in the dim glare of uptown, dreaming of glaciers. Just because I'm a poet, animals and trees think I'm available at all hours of day or night. I don't have a moment to myself."

Later, I found the squirrel staggering across a lawn and cursing to himself. I brought him to my apartment, where I bandaged his head and fed him a big supper, and we talked most of the night. "My relations with poets have been quite warm, as a rule," he told me. "I've been invited any number of times to lecture to their classes on the so-called pathetic fallacy. But this isn't the first time one of them has beaned me. And, strangely, it's always one of the 'nature poets,' who are supposed to be good listeners, who reaches for a rock when I open my mouth. You'd think I'd learn to keep things to myself."

He seemed to be a very bright and promising squirrel, and I'm sure we'll hear a lot more from him in the future.

LOCAL FAMILY
KEEPS SON HAPPY

What happens when parents buy a woman for their sixteen-year-old son? Even in this "swinging" age, such an arrangement would seem to violate most commonly held moral standards. Not so, say Mr. and Mrs. Robert Shepard, of 1417 Swallow Lane.

Two months ago, the Shepards obtained the parole of a twenty-four-year-old prostitute from the County Detention Farm. The woman came to work for the Shepards as a live-in companion for their son, Robert, Jr.

"Robbie had seemed restless and unhappy all last summer," says Mrs. Shepard, a short, neat woman. "He was too young to get a job, and we were afraid he would take up drugs or smoking and drinking. We didn't want him staying out late with the car and taking part in reckless activities. We thought it would be safer to give him what all boys want."

The woman, whose name is Dorothy, is a shapely brunette who could easily pass for eighteen.

"Our boy has matured greatly in the few short weeks since Dorothy came to work for us," says Mr. Shepard, forty-eight, who is an electronics engineer. "He is more poised and more relaxed."

"We see more of him this way, since he stays home evenings and weekends," adds Mrs. Shepard.

Despite the Shepards' success with Dorothy, none of their neighbors have bought women for their sons. For one thing, the cost is prohibitive for many families; Dorothy's wages come to $75 per week, plus room and board.

How does Robbie feel about his new friend?

"At first, I was nervous and keyed-up," he says. "I didn't know what to expect. Gradually, I got used to it and settled down."

In addition to her other duties, Dorothy also cooks breakfast. One of her specialties is "fancy eggs."

FANCY EGGS

6 eggs	$1/2$ cup chopped green pepper
1 cup chopped onion	1 cup tomato sauce

Fry the eggs over easy. Before the eggs become firm, add onion and green pepper. Pour tomato sauce over the eggs and season to taste. Serve hot with corn bread and coffee.

OYA LIFE THESE DAYS

1. The Oya people is the bunch that lives in the Oya Valley, as the neighbors will quickly tell you if you go looking for Oya in the hills. "We are not Oya!" the neighbors shout through locked screen doors. "We are decent, hardworking people, who hardly deserve this."

2. By "this" they mean the Oya custom of going visiting and remaining behind after their ride has left. Apparently, Oya, whose name means "The Us," do not distinguish between themselves and others, and anyone they meet is assumed to be one of them, or one of "The Us," and therefore interested in their comfort and anxious to see that they have enough to eat. But if that person fails to show interest, Oya don't become angry. They wait. Soon enough, they believe, they'll be asked to stay.

3. To the visiting scholar with a keen interest in Oya ways*
and plenty of money to pay for doughnuts, this facet of Oya
life seems harmless and even gentle, but to the neighbors, who
have their own row to hoe, it is known as "the Oya problem."
This refers to the difficulty of conversing with Oya.

4. An Oya converses by means of questions, if at all. His
opening remark might be "That's quite the deal, isn't it?" if
his host is busy, or "Not too busy today, huh?" if the host is
relaxing. Next, he might well ask, "What do you have in your
hand there? A sharp stick?" for by this time the host has realized
that he is in for a long afternoon unless he takes stern measures.
He must at all costs drive the Oya off before he is asked, "What
is the matter? Why don't you like me?"

5. It's impossible to answer that last question in a way that
will satisfy an Oya. Because he doesn't dislike himself, hostility
only makes him curious; he wants to know what he can do to
make the host feel better, such as putting an arm around him.
Right here is where most personal Oya injuries occur—here
and, back home, falling out of bed.

6. Why are Oya disliked so intensely by their neighbors?
The neighbors, who are godly persons, have tried to find the
answer to this one themselves. Prayer meetings are held frequently to discover the Lord's will in regard to the Oya problem.
It is a hard matter. Clearly, the guiding principle should be
"Love thy Oya as thyself," but how can one do that, many ask,
when Oya behave as if they *are* thyself?

---

*Despite their keen interest, scholars have learned practically nothing about the Oya
(pronounced "O-yah"), because of the Oya's equally keen interest in them. Whenever
a research team arrives in the valley, normal activity (if there is such a thing) ceases as
the Oya gather around and watch intently. If the scholars ask, "But what do you *do*?"
the answer is "What would *you* like to do?" or "It's all right, we can always do that
later." Occasionally, the scholars amuse their audience with a short talk, which seems
to be much appreciated. But the Oya never seem to get around to just being themselves.
Some Oya, apparently anxious to please the visitors, may sit on a stump engrossed in
thought, but only a few, and never for longer than a few hours.

7. And such, it seems, is the case. An Oya is quite capable of showing up on Tuesday morning and staying until Sunday night, sitting in your chair, walking beside you through the garden, eating at your table, and not saying anything you'd be able to recall a few minutes later. It is said that the Oya believes that since you and he are both of "The Us," it is the same as if you were alone. And some neighbors say that during an Oya visit they have come to believe this, too—that they are talking to themselves.

8. It is hard to say definitely what Oya believe, however. One can only make suppositions, based on statements of our own that no Oya has seen fit to contradict (e.g., "You don't seem to be in a big rush to leave"). Many younger people in the neighborhood have come to believe that Oya have re-examined the concept of individuality and found it wanting, that Oya have attained loss of self. No Oya has disagreed with this.

9. It may be true that the Oya have much to teach us, but, unless we are mistaken, they have not done so up to the present. They seem to feel it is all the same to them one way or the other. After a visit to an Oya home, one comes away with the feeling they may be right.

10. The Oya personality has been described in conflicting terms. One aspect of it is bliss. Oya seem to have a knack for being "knocked out" by ordinary phenomena, such as a faucet dripping, motes of dust in a beam of light, or the sound of their own throats clearing. It is enough for them if an afternoon brings a light breeze to stir the leaves. This attribute may help to explain their inability to socialize. When spoken to by another, an Oya is fascinated by the speaker's lips.

11. The other essential Oya characteristic is "politeness." An unspoken Oya rule is "Let's wait and see what everyone wants to do." The result is that Oya spend hours waiting, lose track of time, and fall asleep early, missing their favorite programs.

12. Sleep is an ever-present danger, for a strange facet of Oya life is the high number of strenuous sleepers. All Oya thrash about to some extent (some have been known to rise from their beds and strip wallpaper), but many must actually be tied down, lest they get up in their sleep and walk away. The sleeper's family is reluctant to restrain him, or uses only a very light string, and the resulting departures account for the diminishing Oya population in the valley. Someday, it seems, there will be no Oya left here. This prospect neither saddens nor pleases them. It seems that they cannot conceive of a place with no Oya, and they have made no plans to assure that anybody stays around.

YOUR TRANSIT COMMISSION

Your Transit Commission is moving ahead. Hundreds of brand-new buses in bright fresh colors, a brand-new approach to maintenance, plus some brand-new *concepts* in urban transit—they all point to a brand-new *transit experience* for you, the transit consumer.

Maybe you hate mass transit.

Maybe you associate mass transit with surly drivers, exhaust odors, dingy ripped seats with slimy stuff spilled on them, and sickening obscenities scrawled in plain view, filthy windows and paper-littered aisles, standing shoulder-to-shoulder with silent embittered persons and hostile teenagers lugging big ear-busting radios and tape decks, and sudden stops and lurches that send them all crashing and sprawling on top of you! Nightmares of sharp turns by a crazed driver—the mass sways, tilts, slides. You are swept away, pressed against disgusting surfaces by immense bodies—thrown into intimate physical contact with utter strangers who don't care that much for you, either!

Legitimate fears, obsessions. "Bus-riding is the ultimate test of democracy," someone once said. Maybe it was you.

If it was, you haven't seen us *lately*.

Your Transit Commission is more than just a transit commission. It is a total urban transit delivery system. The old days of transit are behind us. We've turned the corner. We aren't what you think we are! We are something entirely different!

Get on the bus. Notice something different? Maybe it's the driver's designer uniform. No more dull khaki or olive drab. Our drivers have come alive in shocking pinks, brilliant blues, dazzling yellows and greens, dynamite reds and oranges. What's more, your driver's uniform is coordinated to the overall design concept of your bus. Each bus on the line is unique—each individually conceptualized by a well-known designer! One bus incorporates a *Star Wars* theme. Another employs a midwestern small-town motif. Another employs linear and spatial relationships in startlingly new and yet ultimately valid ways. One is done in leather. Another is a living Edward Hopper painting.

No more institutional colors! We've made bus-riding an experience that engages the senses! You will find that you can't *wait* for your bus to come!

Get on the bus. Notice the cleaning lady pushing her cleaning-lady cart up and down the aisle. Swabbing, sweeping, mopping, scraping, vacuuming, humming to herself. Candy wrappers are sucked up the moment they hit the deck. Graffiti disappear before the ink is dry. Windows sparkling clean. Ripped seats mended. Air freshened. Back and forth she goes, cleaning each seat as it is vacated. "I will have your seat ready for you in just a moment, sir," she says.

While you are waiting, notice the full-color brochures in the rack behind the driver's seat. Take one. The brochure describes your Transit Commission. It describes the route of your bus, scenic and historic points to look for along the way, noteworthy events in the history of the route, famous people who have ridden along the route, plus data on the typical rider of today— a socio-economic profile, voting patterns, public opinions—*and* a bio of your driver. Stuff you might not have guessed from looking at the back of your driver's head.

> —One is a colonel (ret.) U.S.M.C.
> —Many collect rare coins and stamps.
> —Two are poets.
> —One is a nudist.
> —More than fifty are Episcopalians.

Your Transit Commission wants to make bus-riding personal. We've taken down that old "Unnecessary Conversations" sign. We *want* you to talk with your driver, to exchange ideas and offer insights and share experiences. So introduce yourself! And pour yourself a complimentary cup of coffee from the urn just below the cash box. It's brewed fresh hourly!

"New concepts?" you say. "That's nothing new. That's just old-fashioned neighborliness."

But we're not through yet.

Meet the Affinity Bus.

Why take the first bus that comes along when a bus full of folks who *share your interests* is coming along a moment or two later? The Book Bus, for example, with its lively intelligent well-read ridership, or the Senior Bus, or the Teen Bus. Ethnic Minority Buses with drivers in colorful native dress. Encounter Buses with probing participants who demand honesty, who will stop the bus and sit there and wait for you to come clean. Support Buses. Disco Buses. Upwardly Mobile Buses with compartments instead of seats (complete with tiny sinks, mirrors, plug-ins for shavers or blow-combs). A Runners Bus.

We're proud of that one because we designed it ourselves. We put the seats in the middle where the aisle used to be and a running track around the seats where the seats used to be (moving stanchions hold the runners in and prevent injuries due to vehicle motion—by pushing against the stanchions, the runners generate electricity), enabling you to get in one, two, even three miles on your way to work.

"Good heavens!" you say, "I never dreamed that bus-riding could be like *that*!" But your Transit Commission believes that bus-riding can be *anything we want it to be*! Transit does not have to be a *closed experience*. It can be open-ended. Circular. Expanding. Growing. Dynamic.

We're getting away from the old idea of transit as a means toward an end. The old *linear* idea that has imprisoned transit within a highly structured grid of routes and timetables. We're moving toward a new idea of transit as an experience unto itself, of transit as *pure movement*. The mystique of transit.

Starting tomorrow, your Transit Commission offers the country's first Freedom Bus.

Operating on a different route each morning (selected at random), the Freedom Bus proceeds normally, picking up passengers, until it is almost there—then the driver stops, stands up, and shouts, "Surprise! Surprise, everybody! You're on the Freedom Bus!"

What does that mean? It means that your driver is going to take you for a ride. A whole day of doing nothing but fun things! Instead of going to work or school or the dentist or the I.R.S., you and your companions take off on a day-long excursion. *Free!*

Maybe to the ball park. Maybe to the driver's own home for lunch and a leisurely swim. Maybe to a television quiz show where you might win an all-expenses-paid trip for two to Florida! Maybe a tour of scenic and historic points or a tour of homes of famous persons, such as Gloria Mundi, who will invite the whole bunch of you in to spend the entire afternoon. And as she says goodbye to all of you, maybe she will take you aside personally and say, "You know, a famous person like myself never gets to meet real people like yourself on a one-to-one basis, and this has been a very rewarding experience for me, and I would like to see a lot more of you in the future. Don't hesitate to call me up on the telephone."

One morning, you'll get on the bus as usual and then suddenly you'll get carried away! Lifted up, transported to places you never dreamed you'd be going to. Now that's *transit*.

BE CAREFUL

The anxious weeks and days before the fall of the Skylab satellite certainly did focus new attention on the age-old problem of safety, as millions scanned the skies, dreading the descent of the enormous deadly object. Many tons of metal chunks, some with sharp edges, hurtling earthward, God knew where! Most of us must have been reminded that danger remains America's number one safety problem, and perhaps a few were moved to check their own homes for hazards, for although some dangers can't be completely eliminated—such as a ton of lead heated red-hot by atmospheric friction dropping out of a clear blue sky and crushing your house to smithereens and leaving only a blackened hole in the ground for "Eyewitness News" to show where, moments before, you and your family had been pursuing leisure-time activities—there are dangers we *can* eliminate. These are things we have been warned against time and time again, and you would think people would learn, but do they? No.

For example, the number of persons who put their hands on hot objects annually would stagger you. "Don't touch it, it's hot," the waitress cautions as she places the steaming casserole on the table, and what do people do? They grab hold. Dumb? You bet, and yet you see people doing dumb things every day, and not just kids either but men and women with college degrees earning twenty-five to forty thousand dollars per year.

Item: A famous physicist whose research is so advanced that only two other persons in the world know the first thing about it walks straight out into traffic, thinking it is "smart" to thread his way among speeding cars and buses. They jam on their brakes, just in time, or heedlessly continue to race by, only inches away from his body!

Item: A famous surgeon, one of the very few who knows the human brain like the back of his hand and can go in there and cure unheard-of abnormalities and think nothing of it, places a skilled hand on the head of a strange dog—a tiny terrier, but even small dogs can leap high in the air if their instincts are aroused, and even a friendly pat can arouse them. "Why, he's never done *that* before," the owner says, trying to pull off the pet, whose jaws are clamped on Dr. Thompson's annular ligament.

Item: The editors of a famous newspaper, whose pages are read religiously by world decision-makers daily, lean across a conference table, debating an important editorial that might have far-reaching effects—*and waving sharp copy pencils to emphasize their ideas, as if they were toys!* They aren't. A pencil could poke somebody's eye out, like any other sharp stick.

Yes, many people don't have the sense that God gave geese. They just don't have both oars in the water. Millions of man-hours are spent worrying about the one chance in six hundred billion that immense man-made objects will fall from the sky and cream you; meanwhile, thousands of people wander off every year and get lost in deserted areas.

Stay with the group! You may think that if you get lost a major search will be mounted immediately by the National Guard, using the latest devices, including radar and infrared sensing scanners, but don't count on it. For one thing, you may not be missed: your absence may not be noticed for days or weeks, and even then your friends will figure, "Oh, he'll turn up. He can take care of himself"—even as you wander, helpless and exposed, perhaps only a few yards from a road or a house. And even when the National Guard does come, it doesn't bring sensing devices. These are needed for national defense. If the Guard used its full arsenal of devices every time somebody got lost in this country, the Russians could walk right up Fifth Avenue without a shot being fired. No, the National Guard in this situation is just a bunch of guys beating the bushes, probably miles away from where you've wandered. But *don't wander! Stay put!* Of course, if you had stayed put, you wouldn't have gotten lost in the first place. So (assuming you will walk) don't walk straight, because you will wind up walking in circles. Bear to the right.

Don't eat wild plants, roots, berries, etc. People have been told a thousand times not to put strange things in their mouths, and yet as a result of the environmental movement many assume that anything natural is good and won't hurt them. The best rule: Don't eat it. If you do, spit it out.

Eating itself, especially fish, is a danger area most people overlook completely, thinking, I won't choke, it can't happen to *me*. And yet every week we read about men and women just like ourselves dining in fancy restaurants and choking, which should be a lesson to the rest of us. Indeed, after a big choke scare you will sometimes see restaurant patrons cutting their food into smaller pieces, but they soon forget, and sometimes they go right on eating big forkfuls even as fruitless resuscitation efforts proceed a few feet away.

What is choking like? Those who have experienced it describe it as "the most humiliating thing that ever happened to me." There they are, paying good money for this food and having a wonderful time, talking and joking with close associates, when suddenly, still laughing, they feel the last bite go down the wrong way. Immediately, they sense the foolishness of the situation—to strangle on your own humor!—and they laugh harder and turn red and begin to die, surrounded by people who politely look away. Their obituary flashes before their eyes:

GUY CHOKES ON BEEF, DIES ON FLOOR

Bystander attempts back-pounding procedure, but to no avail. "He was a good eater," say victim's friends, "and a great kidder."

The only hope is that Dr. Henry J. Heimlich, the discoverer of the famous lifesaving anti-choking embrace, will be dining at the same restaurant and will come running over and perform the maneuver on the spot. And yet, to be hugged from behind by a complete stranger while you lie gagging on the floor: Is it worth it? How much better to be smart and not choke at all!

Remember, then: *Eat slowly, take small bites, and don't talk with food in your mouth.* How slowly? Very slowly, say experts. You don't have to dawdle or pick at your food, but do chew thoroughly. Don't "wash it down" with water. Chew it. Twenty times is a good rule for vegetables; for meat, thirty or forty is more like it. Fishbones are the real killers. You should shred the fish, remove all bones, and then follow each bite (small) with a bite of potato or bread, just in case. Better yet, avoid fish.

If, inadvertently, you should choke, don't panic. Stay where you are and motion for assistance. Don't jump up and run. This puts additional strain on the throat, which already has all it can handle.

Running itself is a danger area often pooh-poohed in the cause of "exercise" and "fitness," and yet the increase in running is leading to more and more cases of (1) tripping over things, (2) bumping into things, and (3) falling down.

Don't run. Walk. Facts show that walking for exercise is just as good as running and is much safer, particularly in the dark, on uneven ground, near busy streets, or in the house. Never run in the house, especially if you're tall. It's just plain dumb. And yet every year thousands of tall persons dash headlong into low doorways, decorative overhangs, and light fixtures.

Watch where you're going. Many feel it's a sign of shame to watch their feet while walking, and so keep their eyes straight ahead and "walk tall." They're looking for trouble.

Some falls can't be prevented. The victim is standing perfectly still and then suddenly—*ker blam!*—he's flat on his keister. Researchers say this may be due to a disturbance of the inner ear or to a simple lack of attention, but they don't really know for sure. Injury can be minimized, however, by keeping the feet well apart, the weight well balanced, and the arms slightly extended from the body. A few falls are caused by being cross-eyed, and nothing can be done about those, either. These people were warned about crossing their eyes for fun while in school, but they went ahead and did it anyway. Now they will just have to live with it.

A little common sense is our major weapon against danger. They say that if people would just *stop* and *think* the chance of accidents would be slashed dramatically. Perhaps the spectre of Skylab hanging over our heads might have knocked some sense into people, even though it fell harmlessly into the Atlantic and Indian oceans and parts of Australia, but probably not.

Chances are you will have read this article in very poor light. You knew it was wrong but you went right ahead and did it anyway. What can I tell you that hasn't been said a thousand times before?

TEN STORIES FOR MR. RICHARD BRAUTIGAN, AND OTHER STORIES

Ten stories for Mr. Richard Brautigan are nothing. He never eats lunch until he's thought up one hundred ten. Of these, more than forty are quite good and some are amazing in the way they create a mood or depict a paragraph in just a few words.

BELIEVE IT OR NOT

Some of his stories are no longer than this.

COAL BARGES

His stories are about himself and his own personal life. One day, for example, he wakes up certainly enjoying this bright San Francisco, California, morning with the sun shining directly into his eyes from 94 million miles away and lying near him a beautiful woman whose snores sound exactly like soapy water draining from the bathtub in 1938, and all he has to do is write it down.

My own life would make a pretty dull story, I think, and I envy him as I drive to work on a cold Minnesota morning across the Mississippi River with its coal barges still struggling upstream like so many of us nowadays.

A DULL STORY

Yesterday I needed a little money more than anything else at the moment, so I decided to drive to Sears, where I had bought a new battery last week and been promised $4 for my old one whenever I could bring it in. I put the old battery in the trunk and headed west on Lake Street. (How do you like it so far?) After a few blocks, I picked up a young fellow with a transistor radio playing golden oldies who said after a selection he especially liked for its good beat, "I'm going to my girlfriend's house to get my car, which I've given her the use of for too long now." Later, he added that her house wasn't far from Sears. Half a mile from there, my car ran out of gas. I had two dimes and three pennies in my pocket at the time, so I was naturally relieved when he said he'd go get his car and come back for me.

Shortly he returned behind the wheel of a white Lincoln Continental belonging to her father who was a florist. He explained that his car wouldn't start but that we could wait at her house for her to come home from the movies and pay him the $7 she owed him so he could call a tow truck to give him a push and he'd take me to Sears to get my money so I would be able to buy gas.

We came to her house, which, in fact, was one block away from Sears where the $4 was waiting for me. Her father was quivering anxiously at the curb as if he had been standing there since V-E Day. We got out and he got into the car and drove away, with my old battery in the trunk of that Lincoln Continental.

At the time it seemed better not to mention this unless I wanted to get into the thing even deeper. So I went into the house with the young fellow who was still listening to the radio, and we watched the United States Figure Skating Championships on TV for a while. "May I use your telephone?" I asked during a commercial.

I'll Be Brief

To make a long story short, I called up a friend of mine who said of course he would lend me the money.

$141.38 Altogether

The woman brought Mr. Brautigan a cup of orange-pekoe tea and several letters which she put on the floor beside his bed. In the letters, though he didn't know it then for he was still sleeping soundly, were checks for $20.00, $5.00, and $116.38.

Three Chapters Left out of "A Dull Story"

1. The Junior Ladies runner-up glided to the side of the rink where her parents sat proudly with her arms extended as if she would really like to have lunch with them one of these days.

2. With the little radio clamped to the side of his head, it made a perfect picture of the sort of person you meet now and then who isn't afraid to say what he likes more than your company.

3. On the telephone message pad was written "Janice/ Bob called twice/ this morning. Call/ him at home." I threw it in

the garbage bag. Twice is not many, let's see how much more he wants to be her friend.

LINCOLN TUNNEL

"Wake up! Wake up! You'll be late for work!" a woman was saying early this morning into my ear where I'd left it on the pillow a few hours before. It reminded me of one time driving east when I fell asleep in Harrisburg, Pennsylvania, and woke up in the Lincoln Tunnel. My friend who was at the wheel was saying, "I don't understand why she hasn't spoken to me since Saturday when she knew how much I love her."

SUNNY STREETS

In school we were all taught to develop a character by introducing seemingly unresolvable conflicts into the story which would permit the character to show what sort of stuff he was made of.

What is the conflict or conflicts in these stories? Which of the characters do you identify with the most? Me? Or Mr. Brautigan?

Myself, I identify with Mr. Brautigan. I think he'd be a lot of fun to spend an afternoon with on a long walk along the sunny streets of his favorite city.

IS THIS ALL RIGHT?

Would you mind if I stopped here and went back over these to see what else they may mean that I wasn't aware of at the time?

5

AFTER A FALL

When you happen to step off an edge you didn't see and lurch forward into space waving your arms, it's the end of the world for a second or two, and after you do land, even if you know you're O.K. and no bones are broken, it may take a few seconds to decide whether this is funny or not. Your body is still worked up about the fall—especially the nervous system and the adrenaline-producing areas. In fact, I am *still* a little shaky from a spill that occurred two hours ago, when I put on a jacket, walked out the front door of this house here in St. Paul, Minnesota, and for no reason whatever took a plunge down five steps and landed on the sidewalk flat on my back with my legs in the air. I am thirty-nine years old and in fairly good shape, not prone to blackouts or sudden dizziness, and so a sudden inexplicable fall comes as a big surprise to me.

A woman who was jogging down the street—a short, muscular young woman in a gray sweatshirt and sweatpants—stopped and asked if I was O.K. "Yeah! Fine!" I said and got right up. "I just fell, I guess," I said. "Thanks," I said. She smiled and trotted away.

Her smile has followed me into the house, and I see it now as a smirk, which is what it was. She was too polite to bend over and hoot and shriek and guffaw and cackle and cough and whoop and wheeze and slap her thighs and stomp on the ground, but it was all there in the smile: a young woman who through rigorous physical training and feminist thinking has gradually been taking charge of her own life and ridding her attic of self-hatred and doubt and fear and mindless competitiveness and other artifacts of male-dominated culture is rewarded with the sight of a middle-aged man in a brown suit with a striped tie falling down some steps as if someone had kicked him in the pants.

I'm sorry if I don't consider this humorous. I would like to. I wish she had come over and helped me up and then perhaps sat on the steps with me while I calmed down. We might have got to talking about the fall and how each of us viewed it from a different perspective: that she perceived it as symbolic political theatre, whereas I saw it as something that was actually happening to me at the time. She might have admitted that when she saw me emerge from the house she immediately thought, He earns sixty thousand a year, his secretary earns twelve thousand, and once a year he takes her out to lunch and tells her how much he sympathizes with the women's movement and what a liberating influence it has had on him personally. I might have understood that the sight of a tall man in a suit folding up and waving his arms and falling helplessly and landing flat on his back was the punch line of a joke she had been carrying around with her for a long time.

I might have seen it her way, but she ran down the street,

and now I can only see my side of the fall. I feel old and achy and ridiculous and cheapened by the whole experience. I understand now why my son was so angry with me a few months ago when he tripped on a shoelace and fell in the neighbor's yard—a yard where the neighbor's sheep dog had lived for years—and I cackled at him.

"It's not funny!" he yelled.

"Oh, don't be so sensitive," I said.

Don't be so sensitive! What a dumb thing to say! Who has the right to tell someone else how to feel? It is the right of the person who falls on the dog droppings to decide for himself or herself how he or she will feel. It's not up to a jury. The fallen person determines whether it's funny or not.

My son and I are both tall fellows, and I suppose tall people are the funniest to see fall, because we try so hard not to. We work hard for our dignity, trying to keep that beanpole straight, keep those daddy longlegs coordinated, keep those big boats from tangling with each other. From a chair through a crowded room to the buffet dinner and back to the chair with a loaded plate is a long route for a tall fellow—a route we have to study for tricky corners and edges, low doorways, light fixtures, rug wrinkles, and other low-lying obstacles that we, being tall, don't see at a glance. A tall fellow has got his hands full on a maneuver like that. He is pulling strings attached to all his joints, knowing that if he lets himself go or makes a mistake, it's a long way down.

Short, compact persons can trip and recover their balance quickly, maybe even turn that stumble into a casual Twyla Tharp–type dance move or a Buster Keaton fall, but when tall fellows stumble they go down like cut timber. We're not like Walter Payton, of the Chicago Bears, who bounces right up from the turf when he's tackled. We're more like the tall trees in the National Basketball Association. When they fall, usually there's ligament damage or torn cartilage; the stretcher crew runs onto the floor, and the crowd applauds sympathetically as the debris is stacked and carried away. "The knee feels good," the tree says six months later. "I am lifting weights with it, and I am now almost able to bend over," but he knows that his pro tree career is done gone, that he has begun a new career as a guy who hurts a lot.

All that can happen in one quick fall, and so a tall fellow is cautious when he threads his way through the party to reload his plate with spareribs. One misstep and down he goes, to the vast amusement of all present, who don't realize that he has wrenched something in his back and will be in a body cast for months and not be so good a friend again. Only a tall fellow knows how major his fall might be.

Five years ago, I got on a bus with five musicians and rode around for two weeks doing shows every night. They played music; I told jokes and sang a song. One night, in the cafeteria of a junior college in southern Minnesota, we happened to draw a big crowd, and the stage—four big plywood sheets on three-foot steel legs—was moved back twenty feet to make room for more chairs. The show was late starting, the room was stuffy, the crowd was impatient, and when finally the lights dimmed and the spotlight shone on the plywood, I broke from the back door and made a run for the stage, thinking to make a dramatic entrance and give these fine people the show they were waiting for.

What I could not see in the dark was the ceiling and a low concrete overhang that the stage had been moved partly under, and then the spotlight caught me straight in the eyes and I couldn't see anything. I leaped up onto the stage, and in mid-leap my head hit concrete and my right leg caught the plywood at mid-shin. I toppled forward, stuck out my hands, and landed on my hands and knees. The crowd drew a long breath. I got right up—I had been doing shows long enough to know not to lie onstage and cry in front of a paying audience—and, seeing the microphone about ten feet ahead, strode up to it and held out my arms and said, "Hello, everybody! I'm happy to be here!"

Then they laughed—a big thunderstorm of a laugh and a big round of applause for what they now saw had been a wonderful trick. But it wasn't funny! My neck hurt! I hurt all over! On the other hand, to see a tall man in a white suit jump directly into a ceiling and then fall down—how often does a person get to see that? Men dive off high towers through fiery hoops into tiny tanks, men rev up motorcycles and leap long rows of trucks and buses, but I am the only man in show business who takes a good run and jumps Straight Up Into Solid Concrete Using Only His Bare Head. Amazing!

Let's see that once more in slow motion:

Me in the hallway saying, "Now?" Stage manager saying, "Not yet, not yet," then, "O.K., *now*." He opens door, I take two steps, see bright circle of light on stage, take five long running strides. In mid-run, the circle moves, man is blinded by the light, looks for edge of stage, then leaps—pushing off with left foot, right leg extended. Head hits concrete, stopping upward motion. Forward momentum carries body onto stage but right leg fails to clear plywood. Body falls, lands on hands and knees, stands up—like a dropped puppet picked up by puppeteer—walks forward, speaks. *Laughter & applause.* Looking at this footage one more time, you can see how hard this poor guy hit. The head jerks, the eyes squeeze shut, the hands fly up like birds, the body shudders.

Look now as the tall fellow who has had a load of bricks dropped on his head starts singing. It's a song he has sung for years and knows by heart, so it doesn't matter that he is senseless; these lyrics are stored not in his head but at the lower end of the spinal cord. "Hello, hello, it's time for the show! We're all dressed up and rarin' to go!" But his eyes are glazed, and it's clear that something is terribly wrong. Stop the show! This man is hurt! Is there a doctor in the house? This fellow may have broken his neck! Friends, this entertainer who always gave you everything he had has now given you too much. His life is now shattered, owing to one last effort to jump head first into a ceiling for your pleasure and amazement.

    —You've now seen in slow motion the play that led to the injury that so tragically ended your career. Tell us in your own words, if you can, what goes through your mind as you see yourself jump into the ceiling.
    —Howard, I've tried to put all that behind me. I have no hard feelings toward the guy who moved the stage or the audience that laughed—they were only doing their job. Right now my job is to regain my sense of humor and go back to work. I feel like I'm making real good progress. Howard, I consider myself to be one lucky guy.

Oh, it is a sad story, except for the fact that it isn't. My ceiling jump got the show off to a great start. The band played three fast tunes, and I jumped carefully back onstage and did a monologue that the audience, which now *knew* I was funny, laughed at a lot. Even I, who had a headache, thought it was funny. I really did feel lucky.

So do I still—a tall man who fell now sitting down to write his memoirs. The body is so delicate, the skeleton so skinny; we are stick men penciled in lightly, with a wooden stick cage to protect the heart and lungs and a cap of bone over the brain. I wonder that I have survived so many plunges, so many quick drops down the short arc that leads to the ground.

The Haymow Header of 1949: Was playing in Uncle Jim's haymow and fell through a hole, landing in the bull's feed trough, barely missing the stanchion, and was carried into the house, where Grandma put brown paper on my head. *The Milk Jar Mishap of 1951:* Tripped on the cellar steps while carrying two gallon glass jars full of milk from the grocery, dropped the jars (which broke), and then landed on them but didn't cut myself. Went to my room and cried. My dad said, "That's all right, it doesn't matter." But it did matter. I had ruined us— my poor family! A week's worth of milk gone bust, and it was my fault. *Miscellaneous Bike Bowls, 1954– :* Biking no-handed. Going over the bike jump. Going down a steep hill and hitting loose gravel. Practicing bike skids. Swerving to avoid a dog. *The Freshman Composition Class Collapse of 1960:* After staying up all night to write an essay on a personal experience, rose in Mr. Cody's class to read it, blacked out, and fell on top of people sitting in front of me. Got up and went home. *Miscellaneous Sports Spills:* Basketball collision that dislocated left elbow in 1961. Skating, skiing, tobogganing. Two memorable outfield collisions, after one of which a spectator said she could hear our heads hit two hundred and fifty feet away.

Falls of Fatherhood: Walking across the room, thinking long-range thoughts. Suddenly there's an infant at my feet, whom I am just about to step on! And instantly I lift the foot and dive forward, sometimes catching myself short of a fall and sometimes doing a half gainer into the furniture. (I also fall for cats.) *The Great Ladder Leap of 1971:* Climbing up to install a second-story storm window, felt the extension ladder slip to one side, dropped the window and jumped, landing in a flower bed, barely missing my two-year-old boy standing nearby. *Dreams of Falls:* Too numerous, too common, to mention. Always drawn toward the edge by some powerful force, tumble through space, then wake up and go get a glass of water.

The first time I ever went naked in mixed company was at the
house of a girl whose father had a bad back and had built himself
a sauna in the corner of the basement. Donna and I were friends
in college. Both of us had grown up in fundamentalist Christian
homes, and we liked to compare notes on that. We both felt
constricted by our upbringings and were intent on liberating
ourselves and becoming more free and open and natural. So it
seemed natural and inevitable one night to wind up at her house
with some of her friends there and her parents gone and to take
off our clothes and have a sauna.

We were nineteen years old and were very cool ("Take off
my clothes? Well, sure. Heck, I've taken them off *dozens* of
times") and were careful to keep cool and be nonchalant and
not look at anybody below the neck. We got into the sauna as
if getting on the bus. *People do this*, I thought to myself. *There
is nothing unusual about it! Nothing! We all have bodies! There is
no reason to get excited! This is a normal part of life!*

We filed into the little wooden room, all six of us, avoiding
unnecessary body contact, and Donna poured a bucket of water
on the hot rocks to make steam. It was very quiet. "There's a
shower there on the wall if you want to take a shower," she
said in a strange, nervous voice.

"Hey! How about a shower!" a guy said in a cool-guy voice,
and he turned on the water full blast. The shower head leaped
from the wall. It was a hand-held type—a nozzle at the end of
a hose—and it jumped out at us like a snake and thrashed
around exploding ice-cold water. He fell back, someone screamed,
I slipped and fell, Donna fell on top of me, we leaped apart,
and meanwhile the nozzle danced and flew from the force of the
blast of water. Donna ran out of the sauna and slipped and fell
on the laundry-room floor, and another girl yelled, "God damn
you, Tom!" Donna scrambled to her feet. "God! Oh, God!" she

cried. Tom yelled, "I'm sorry!" Another guy laughed a loud, wicked laugh, and I tiptoed out as fast as I could move, grabbed my clothes, and got dressed. Donna grabbed her clothes. "Are you all right?" I said, not looking at her or anything. "No!" she said. Somebody laughed a warm, appreciative laugh from inside the sauna. "Don't laugh!" she yelled. "It isn't funny! It isn't the least bit funny!"

"I'm *not* laughing," I said, though it wasn't me she was angry at. I *still* am not laughing. I think it's a very serious matter, twenty years later. Your first venture as a naked person, you want it to go right and be a good experience, and then some joker has to go pull a fast one.

All I can say is, it's over now, Donna. Don't let it warp your life. We were young. We meant well. We wanted to be natural and free. It didn't mean we were awful. God didn't turn on the cold water to punish us for taking off our clothes—Tom did, and he didn't mean it, either. It was twenty years ago. Let's try to forget it. Write me a letter and let me know how you're doing. I would like to hear that you're doing well, as I am, and that our night of carnal surprise did you no lasting harm. Life is so wonderful, Donna. I remember once, after I lost track of you, I ran on the dock of a summer camp where I worked as a counselor—ran and slipped on the wet boards and did a backward half somersault in the air and instead of hitting the dock and suffering permanent injury I landed clean in the water head first and got water up my nose and came up sneezing and choking, but *I was all right*, and is that so surprising? It was luck, I suppose, but then two-thirds of the earth's surface is water, so our chances are not so bad, and when you add in the amount of soft ground, bushes, and cushions in the world and the amazingly quick reactions of the body to protect itself, I think the odds of comedy are better than even. God writes a lot of comedy, Donna; the trouble is, He's stuck with so many bad actors who don't know how to play funny. When I dropped the window off that falling ladder back in 1971, I didn't know that my son had come around the corner of the house and was standing at the foot of the ladder watching me. The window hit the ground and burst, the ladder hit the ground and bounced, and his father landed face first in the chrysanthemums; all three missed him by a few feet. Quite a spectacle for a little boy to see up close, and he laughed out loud and clapped his hands. I moved my arms to make sure they weren't broken into little pieces, and I clapped, too. Hurray for God! So many fiction writers nowadays would have sent the window down on that boy's head as if it were on a pulley and the rope were around his neck, but God let three heavy objects fall at his feet and not so much as scratch him. He laughed to see me and I laughed to see him. He was all right and I wasn't so bad myself.

I haven't seen you since that night, Donna. I've told the sauna story to dozens of people over the years, and they all thought it was funny, but I still don't know what you think. Are you all right?

THE DRUNKARD'S SUNDAY

The drunk man walks carefully and (he imagines) gracefully through three rooms of men and women who observe him, carrying two full glasses of white wine and the wine bottle and placing them on a small table successfully.

He shouldn't have drunk so much, they think. He thinks, they shouldn't have either. It's the middle of the afternoon, and out in the lake, little kids splash and scream whose parents are drunk who should be watching them.

Still, he has managed to walk through three rooms of a crowd watching him and to feel almost like a dancer doing it.

Fred Astaire had a few drinks, and he'd get up and dance across the floor and up the wall, he'd dance on the sofa and tip it over and dance it back up again and make it look terrific. William Powell and Myrna Loy, they'd get up and make a drink like you'd get up and turn on a lamp. Cary Grant would say,

"Darling, fix me a drink." Humphrey Bogart, Clark Gable, Elizabeth Taylor, John Wayne, Tracy and Hepburn—everybody except Charlton Heston.

It's the drunk man's party, and now he'd like to go to sleep and wake up and it'd be ten o'clock that morning again. He'd sit on the porch swing with his little daughter and let her tell him things, *O Daddy Daddy my Daddy*, her little hand in his big one.

Tears come into his eyes. The woman who is talking to him is saying that she and her husband are thinking of buying a pontoon houseboat, one big enough to sleep at least four but small enough to be towed on a trailer, but she sees his tears and excuses herself to go to the kitchen. The drunk man excuses himself to a chair to go out the door and out the driveway into the woods.

Away from the house, he cries a little more. His chest begins to heave and his face is contorted with sobs. Pictures come to mind:

> His daughter drowns, he is divorced, his mother dies, and he is struck by a car and crippled for life; his daughter drowns and his wife drowns too—his mother and father both die, they are shot—and he becomes a drunken bum who sleeps in boxcars and is drunk by noon and falls down on the sidewalk and pees on himself; his daughter drowns because he was too drunk to swim out and save her, and his wife divorces him in disgust and never speaks to him again—neither does his mother—his father shoots himself.

The drunk man walks far into the woods and out into a meadow of sweet clover, birds, good dirt, but he is so sweaty, so bit up and sadly drunk, that nothing here can make him feel better or change his mind: that he is a stupid man and unforgivable fool and a miserable son-of-a-bitch, and that this is only the beginning of a long road that leads through the woods into town past the school, the courthouse, the V.F.W., the lumberyard, the town dump, past the abandoned train station into the weeds to the boxcar.

He turns around and walks home. The cars are gone. Everyone is gone except his daughter and his wife. The little girl sings along with the television set, and he puts his arms around the good and handsome woman who has cleared away the glasses, bottles, napkins, and filthy ashtrays and picked up the cheese, cold cuts, chips, sour cream, herring, bean dip, sliced carrots, celery, peppers, cauliflower, radishes, and pickles and fixed a cup of beef soup for his supper and who puts her arms around him and is glad to see him.

He takes a shower and puts on clean shirt and slacks. Barefoot, he has supper with her gratefully. She laughs about the party. They watch "60 Minutes." They sit on the porch swing. The sun goes down. She hears birds and identifies each of them. The little girl crawls into her lap, and she tells her a story about a fish who crawls out of the lake when the moon is full and walks on legs and sings like Barry Manilow, "I wish, I wish, that I was not a fish."

The drunk man is not drunk now and he will never be drunk again. He will love his wife and child and work hard at things he does well to earn more money so that he can give them all the good things they want:

Trips to Europe, West Africa, India, Japan, and all around the world; a wonderful old house with a screened-in veranda, fireplace, full dining room, big bedrooms with bay windows and twelve-foot ceilings, a kitchen as big as a living room, a bathroom with a tub as big as a dinghy; books, cameras, camping equipment, barbecue grill, records, clothes, expensive original paintings, color television, tickets to movies and shows and concerts, dinners in expensive restaurants—Northern Italian, Provincial French, Szechuan Chinese, South American and Mexican, Jewish.

He isn't drunk; in fact, his mind is clearer than it's been all day. He feels like his day is just starting. It's getting late but he just keeps feeling better. He's going to call his mother and father in California and write a letter to his sister and brother-in-law in Houston; he's going to sit down and make a list of chores that he has let slide around here since spring; and then he's going to go upstairs and lie down and make love with his wife with a heart full of passionate devotion. Finally, he will get dressed and come downstairs and draw a floor plan of that house.

And that's just for starters. He may stay up all night!

He may stay up and work and then fix pancakes for breakfast and work all day tomorrow.

This just may be the turning point in what had seemed to be a hopeless story about one man's eventual ruin. If this house were the world, this would be the point at which men finally decided to set things straight:

> To work, to love, to be handsome and gentle and useful, and to make peace with themselves; to put aside vain strivings and prepare for the Kingdom of God; when nation shall no longer be set against nation nor man against man; when hatred and fear are no longer in them; when their minds shall be filled with understanding and their souls with lovingkindness.

No sooner does he think this than the drunk man feels all of it pass away from him; he is alone on the swing, his wife and daughter have gone upstairs, and he feels weaker than he has felt all day. His stomach hurts.

Actually, it is a pain just above the stomach. It is a sharp pain, not excruciating but more than an ache, and it begins just above the stomach and goes up into the chest.

It seems to come and go. When it comes again, he considers calling Dr. Humphreys but it's late, the doctor would call the ambulance, and he'd be driven into town to spend the night in the hospital with tubes in his arms and nose and wires taped to his chest, and sleep, half-awake, listening to nurses walking around, and names being paged over speakers in the ceiling.

He stands up slowly and walks carefully through the quiet house and up the stairs, turning lights off behind him, and into the bedroom where his wife is sleeping, and lies down in his clothes and goes to sleep himself.

HAPPY TO BE HERE

I know of several writers who sought paradise diligently, in hopes that it held a vivid description that might form the basis for several lasting poetic masterpieces. They found instead that paradise, for them, was like:

> A beautiful experience.
> Being present at the Creation.
> Really great.
> Nothing I ever experienced before.

And they were, like:

> Overcome with wonder.
> Real glad I came.
> Sorry I can't stay longer.

Disappointed by similes no more wonderful or beautiful than those inspired by hard liquor, most of these individuals later turned against paradise and said it was nothing (which, of course, it is, as well as being everything), and said they would never go back again. And they haven't, choosing to remain in the city of doubt and confusion.

When I moved to a farm one year ago, I didn't think much of it. I had learned from the experience of others not to expect a sudden attack of delight upon arrival, or words falling over themselves to get put on paper. My first thought—"Here I am"—said enough, I think, without trying to wring something like ecstasy out of what is an ordinary Minnesota farm (hogs, beef cattle, feed grains). Understand, however, that I was aware of paradise being there, and meant to have a look at it. I thought that dawn would be the right time. As I'm not an early riser by nature, I was sure any sunrise I witnessed would be one that God had called me to see and provided me words to describe.

In order to be ready for that moment, I set out to rid myself of a sneaky city prose style, which was the result of my years of striving to be tops in the novel. Before I retired to quiet country life, my ambition had been to write a novel every two years. To facilitate this outpouring of the spirit, I had trained myself to *think* the novel, mentally narrating passages of my daily life in fictional fashion. For example, while showering I might be thinking, "The warm water struck the back of his neck and streamed down his body, reawakening in him the old desire for Catherine." When the telephone rang, I'd think, "He hesitated inwardly—a barely perceptible moment of doubt that, as his fingers touched the cold metal, was overcome by his need to talk with someone, even a complete stranger." I turned my life into one long interior monologue, putting myself through the wringer in order to make my novels more realistic than my own life happened to be at the time in comparison to novels I

had read. I began to have fears about my capacity to love—
fears that were not mine but my characters'. I was constantly
torn by inner contradictions, although in cold fact I was as smug
as a lizard. When, let us say, I felt a wave of warm tenderness
sweep over me, I didn't know if it was my tenderness or that
of Sammy Delphine, the hero of my novel-in-progress.

I decided that if I kept on being introspective, I was going
to wind up motivating myself right into the ground. I began
sleeping twelve to sixteen hours a day in order to have a little
time by myself. Finally, under the influence of my sleeping life
(in dreams, I was always just sitting around doing nothing), I
moved to the farm.

Out in the sticks, my city self got unwound in a remarkably
short time. I tried keeping a journal, recording various thoughts,
impressions, natural data ("forty-eight animals seen today before
lunch, of which all but six were birds, most small and brown-
ish"), but quit after two pages and sat and waited it out for
nine months and didn't think about my own thoughts so much.
What I was beginning to experience, I later learned, was "the
being of being" that J. W. Spagnum, the prairie transcenden-
talist, describes as "the profound fullness of spirit that renders
the heart immovable." In *The Wisdom of the Plains*, he writes:

> The first and highest paradise is our heavenly home and the
> second is the Garden of Eden, shown on the Chart of Time (inside
> front cover) as a sunny sky and a grove of trees. Life in these
> fabulous places is characterized by emptiness of the heart as we
> know it; i.e., absence of all desire. A third possible paradise is
> certain geographical areas here on earth, such as wide-open spaces
> that turn our attention Upward. By giving ourselves entirely to
> contemplation of this silent world, we may achieve that read-
> justment of perception that we know as innocence.

This year, my readjustment of perception was helped out by
a bad spring cold that kept me indoors for two weeks. Stuffed-

up ears shut me inside my head, a sphere of peaceful quiet, and served to jam all second thoughts I might have had about the silent world of wide-open spaces. I simply couldn't hear myself think. Propped up in bed, I wrote my first plain country prose, "Driving to Town," which I present here, along with three later works, to illustrate how far I had come from city life.

DRIVING TO TOWN

One day while driving to town I was inclined to stop by an old farmer I saw looking over his crop and say, "That's certainly doing well," then realized I didn't know what "that" was. Also it looked burnt.

AUGUST 1ST

August 1st and still a stranger. In the town tavern, having seen Otto do this once, I held up two fingers for a whiskey-and-a-wash and was brought two beers, of which I drank one, the bartender curiously eyeing me and at last asking didn't I want two. I said no, that I had seen Otto hold up two fingers for a whiskey-and-a-wash. He said yes but I have known Otto for thirty years and know what he wants.

ALFRED'S TRACTOR

When the Allis-Chalmers got away from him one day and he had to jump free, Alfred didn't run after it but only stood and watched as the tractor went around and around in wider and wider circles, discing and harrowing the hell out of forty acres of spring wheat until it stopped, out of gas, then said to Edna, "Look at that. She done almost as good a job as if I'd been on her myself."

At Piggott's

Once I went to Piggott's after supper to return the seeder. He and Daryl were in the old saggy barn carrying hay bales from the weak side that had to be braced up underneath to the strong side already braced. I helped carry bales until ten o'clock, cutting up my hands, and didn't get a word of thanks for it. But then, they hadn't asked me to help, of course.

I wrote "At Piggott's" one day in two quick bursts. Writing a story with three characters in it in one day is quick work. I'm pleased with the stories. I don't know if I simplified my life in order to write better or the other way around. I do know that winter, which was long this year and saw a week's thaw in March followed by a cold snap in April, in previous years would have led to feelings of desperation and a longing for release, but this winter didn't. I just felt cold. In the old days of novel-writing, my son's birthday, on May 1st, would have made me think of the coincidence of revolution and spring, the death-rebirth motif. This year it didn't, and we had a good time. He received a sandbox, a tricycle, a toy farm, and a fifty-dollar savings bond. At end of day, I did not find myself brooding about my own sandbox experiences. I went to bed early.

May 2nd: Asleep upstairs with the windows open for the first time in months, I was awake at five or six in the morning. The air was cool and wet. I put on blue striped trousers, a green wool sweater, and blue sneakers. Our dog chuckled in the kitchen, hearing, as I did, the birds, a thousand of them, and I opened the screen door and let us out. What I saw was the old red barn (with cows in it), the granary full of oats, the empty chicken coop, the machine sheds (with rusty parts lying around on the ground outside), the corncribs full of corn, and the pump house, pig barn, and silo, the brown brick house, hundreds of trees, the cow pasture, creek, low swamp, and dump, and beyond the trees, fields plowed last fall that smelled of pig and cow manure, and front and back roads, neighbors' fields and woods, and clear sky.

I walked across the yard and sat on a big rock by the road. I heard the dog bark, four clear barks.

FOUND PARADISE

Found paradise. I said I would and by God I have. Here it is, and it is just what I knew was here all along. Well, I guess that is about it. I'm happy to be here, is all.

DROWNING 1954

When I was twelve, my cousin Roger drowned in Lake Independence, and my mother enrolled me in a swimming class at the Y.M.C.A. on La Salle Avenue in downtown Minneapolis. Twice a week for most of June and July, I got on the West River Road bus near our home in Brooklyn Park township, a truck-farming community north of Minneapolis, and rode into the stink and heat of the city, and when I rounded the corner of Ninth Street and La Salle and smelled the chlorine air that the building breathed out, I started to feel afraid. After a week, I couldn't bear to go to swimming class anymore.

Never before had I stood naked among strangers (the rule in the class was no swimming trunks), and it was loathsome to undress and then walk quickly through the cold showers to the pool and sit shivering with my feet dangling in the water (Absolute Silence, No Splashing) and wait for the dread moment.

The instructor—a man in his early twenties, who was tanned and had the smooth muscles of a swimmer (he wore trunks)— had us plunge into the pool one at a time, so that he could give us his personal attention. He strode up and down the side of the pool yelling at those of us who couldn't swim, while we thrashed hopelessly beneath him and tried to *look* like swimmers. "You're walking on the bottom!" he would shout. "Get your legs up! What's the matter, you afraid to get your face wet? What's *wrong* with you?" The truth was that my cousin's death had instilled in me a terrible fear, and when I tried to swim and started to sink it felt not so much as if I was sinking but as if something was pulling me down. I panicked, every time. It was just like the dreams of drowning that came to me right after Roger died, in which I was dragged deeper and deeper, with my body bursting and my arms and legs flailing against nothing, down and down, until I shot back to the surface and lay in my dark bedroom exhausted, trying to make myself stay awake.

I tried to quit the swimming class, but my mother wouldn't hear of it, so I continued to board the bus every swimming morning, and then, ashamed of myself and knowing God would punish me for my cowardice and deceit, I hurried across La Salle and past the Y and walked along Hennepin Avenue, past the pinball parlors and bars and shoeshine stands to the old public library, where I viewed the Egyptian mummy and the fossils and a facsimile of the Declaration of Independence. I stayed there until eleven-thirty, when I headed straight for the WCCO radio studio to watch "Good Neighbor Time."

We listened regularly to this show at home—Bob DeHaven, with Wally Olson and His Band, and Ernie Garvin and Burt Hanson and Jeanne Arland—and then to the noontime news, with Cedric Adams, the most famous man in the upper Midwest. It amazed me to sit in the studio audience and watch the little band crowded around the back wall, the engineers in the darkened booth, and the show people gliding up to a microphone for a song, a few words, or an Oxydol commercial. I loved everything except the part of the show in which Bob DeHaven interviewed people in the audience. I was afraid he might pick me, and then my mother, and probably half of Minnesota, would find out that I was scared of water and a liar to boot. The radio stars dazzled me. One day, I squeezed into the WCCO elevator with Cedric Adams and five or six other people. I stood next to him, and a sweet smell of greatness and wealth drifted off from him. I later imagined Cedric Adams swimming in Lake Minnetonka—a powerful whale of happiness and purpose—and I wished that I were like him and the others, but as the weeks wore on I began to see clearly that I was more closely related to the bums and winos and old men who sat around in the library and wandered up and down Hennepin Avenue. I tried to look away and not see them, but they were all around me there, and almost every day some poor ragged creature, filthy drunk at noon, would stagger at me wildly out of a doorway, with his arms stretched out toward me, and I saw a look of fellowship in his eyes: *You are one of us.*

I ran from them, but clearly I was well on my way. Drinking and all the rest of the bum's life would come with time, inevitably. My life was set on its tragic course by a sinful error in youth. This was the dark theme of the fundamentalist Christian tracts in our home: one misstep would lead you down into the life of the infidel. One misstep! A lie, perhaps, or disobedience to your mother. There were countless young men in those tracts who stumbled and fell from the path—*one misstep!*—and were dragged down like drowning men into debauchery, unbelief, and utter damnation. I felt sure that my lie, which was repeated twice a week and whenever my mother asked about my swimming, was sufficient for my downfall. Even as I worked at the deception, I marveled that my fear of water should be greater than my fear of Hell.

I still remember the sadness of wandering in downtown Minneapolis in 1954, wasting my life and losing my soul, and my great relief when the class term ended and I became a kid again around the big white house and garden, the green lawns and cool shady ravine of our lovely suburb. A weekend came when we went to a lake for a family picnic, and my mother, sitting on the beach, asked me to swim for her, but I was able to fool her, even at that little distance, by walking on the bottom and making arm strokes.

When I went to a lake with my friends that summer, or to the Mississippi River a block away, I tried to get the knack of swimming, and one afternoon the next summer I did get it—the crawl and the backstroke and the sidestroke, all in just a couple of weeks. I dived from a dock and opened my eyes underwater and everything. The sad part was that my mother and father couldn't appreciate this wonderful success; to them, I had been a swimmer all along. I felt restored—grateful that I would not be a bum all my life, grateful to God for letting me learn to swim. It was so quick and so simple that I can't remember it today. Probably I just stood in the water and took a little plunge; my feet left the bottom, and that was it.

Now my little boy, who is seven, shows some timidity around water. Every time I see him standing in the shallows, working up nerve to put his head under, I love him more. His eyes are closed tight, and his pale slender body is tense as a drawn bow, ready to spring up instantly should he start to drown. Then I feel it all over again, the way I used to feel. I also feel it when I see people like the imperial swimming instructor at the Y.M.C.A.—powerful people who delight in towering over some little twerp who is struggling and scared, and casting the terrible shadow of their just and perfect selves. The Big Snapper knows who you are, you bastards, and in a little while he is going to come after you with a fury you will not believe and grab you in his giant mouth and pull you under until your brain turns to jelly and your heart almost bursts. You will never recover from this terror. You will relive it every day, as you lose your fine job and your home and the respect of your friends and family. You will remember it every night in your little room at the Mission, and you will need a quart of Petri muscatel to put you to sleep, and when you awake between your yellow-stained sheets your hands will start to shake all over again.

You have fifteen minutes. Get changed.